INSIGHT COMPACT GUIDES

SOUTH [

GREAT LITTLE GUIDES

Compact Guide: South Downs is the essential quick-reference guide to one of the favourite holiday regions of southern England. It tells you all you need to know about its attractions, from fun-filled Brighton to Chichester Cathedral and the pictureque villages of Sussex.

This is just one title in *Apa Publications'* new series of pocket-sized, easy-to-use guidebooks intended for the independent-minded traveller. *Compact Guides* pride themselves on being up-to-date and authoritative. They are in essence mini travel encyclopedias, designed to be comprehensive yet portable, as well as readable and reliable.

Star Attractions

An instant reference to some of the South Downs' most popular tourist attractions to help you on your way.

Chichester Cathedral, p18

Palace of Fishbourne, p19

Bosham, p20

Arundel, p27

Brighton, p33

Steyning, p41

Lewes Castle, p45

Anne of Cleves House, p47

Cissbury, p40

Beachy Head, p56

Seven Sisters Country Park, p57

SOUTH DOWNS

Introduction

The South Downs – Hillside and Seaside 5
Historical Highlights 10

Places

Route 1: Chichester and Surroundings 16
Route 2: The West Sussex Downs 21
Route 3: Midhurst and the Rother Valley 25
Route 4: Bognor to Shoreham 29
Route 5: Brighton 33
Route 6: The Central Downs 40
Route 7: Lewes 44
Route 8: Bloomsbury-on-Sea 48
Route 9: Eastbourne 53

Culture

Archaeology 59
Architecture and Art 60
Music and Theatre 63

Leisure

Food and Drink 65
Activity Holidays 68

Practical Information

Getting There 71
Getting Around 72
Facts for the Visitor 74
For Children 77
Accommodation 78

Index 80

The Sussex Downs: Hillside and Seaside

Misty morning on the Downs

The Sussex Downs are one of Britain's most famous landscapes, a haunch of rolling chalk hills that stretches from Eastbourne into Hampshire. This was a high road into England for the early settlers, who started clearing land for farming 6,000 years ago, leaving it crew-cut by sheep and striated by plough shares. On the high spots, where Iron-Age forts and flint mines flourished, the wind whispers through copses, windmill sails and woodland clumps which rise over voluptuous gullies and combes, remnants of the last Ice Age which scooped out devils' dykes and punchbowls. The South Downs Way, a white streamer, clings to the crest, with unceasing views across the Channel coast and, to the north, over the wooded Weald. In 1972 the Countryside Commission declared it the first long distance bridleway in Britain.

Chalk is horribly sticky when wet, which meant that until quite recent times, communications were poor: there is a 17th-century account of a woman needing six oxen to pull her cart to church in Lewes, and in 1702 the king of Spain took six hours to cover the last 9 miles (15km) of a journey to Petworth. For centuries the inland forest of the Weald had been an impenetrable barrier, and South Saxon blood was unmingled with that of the rest of Britain. Christianity arrived here a century after it did at Canterbury, which is less than 50 miles (80km) away, and when it did turn up, in the form of St Wilfred, it came by boat, from Yorkshire.

5

When the roads were eventually in place and the railway established, in the 18th and 19th centuries, the flood gate quickly opened. Fishing villages that sheltered beneath the Downs mushroomed into vast resorts: Sussex by the Sea was the catchy tune, and everyone came to walk along the prom, where the brass bands played *tiddley-om-pom-pom*. The Prince Regent brought a rakishness to Brighton, the Victorians added frivolous piers, and a sense of fun remains.

Prince Regent

Today, some 5 million visit the coast each year, a high percentage of them English, though a cheering number of students come from overseas to study English.

What they find in the coastal resorts is entertainment, good beaches, inexpensive accommodation. What they find just inland, if they bother to look, are some surprisingly rural spots. Drive along the north side of the Downs from Poynnings to Washington, past the great flint manor farms, and feel time slip away; roll over the parklands between Midhurst and Petworth and feel the full grace of the English countryside; stand on the Trundle above the fine natural racecourse at Goodwood and see, miles away, Chichester and the coast.

Goodwood Park

Because water is hard to come by on the top of the Downs, they are happily bereft of urban occupation. Today the large towns are all on the coast. Eastbourne remains a resort for the well-to-do, Brighton continues to be raffish and popular, Worthing may be winning its fight to prove it is not a place for the elderly, and Chichester always seems unfussed by the world which by and large has passed it by. Inland the towns of Midhurst, Petworth, Steyning and Ditchling, with their coaching inns and pubs, tea shops, galleries and antique shops, are the epitome of the quaint English country town. However built up the coast has become, quiet corners of the South Downs are never far away.

Location and size

The South Downs run 100 miles (160km) from Winchester in Hampshire to the Seven Sisters and Beachy Head, the dramatic, crumbling white cliffs rising above the English Channel near Eastbourne: the Sussex Downs occupy the easterly 53 miles. Between 3 and 5 miles (4–8km) wide, they average a height of 600-700ft (180–215m), their highest point being just over the Hampshire border at Buster Hill (889ft/270m): in Sussex, Duncton Down is 837ft (255m), Ditchling Beacon is 813ft (247m) and Chantonbury 783ft (238m).

The county of Sussex, the kingdom of the South Saxons, covers 1,457 square miles (3,773sq km), and is divided into East and West Sussex around the River Ardur just west of Brighton. Chichester, the cathedral town of Sussex, is the county town of West Sussex; Lewes, formerly county town of Sussex, is now the county town of East Sussex.

Formerly the county was divided into six rapes. The rapes were strips of land running inland, each with access to the sea, though their ports were often miles from the coast. Chichester had its own port. The rape of Arundel had Arundel as its port on the Arun which today reaches the sea at Littlehampton. The rape of Bramber on the Adur, which reaches the sea at Shoreham, had a port at Steyning. The rape of Lewes was on the Ouse which today comes out at the Channel port of Newhaven.

There are six small rivers in Sussex (Rother, Levant, Arun, Adur, Ouse and Cuckmere) and none extend beyond the county borders. Shoreham and Newhaven are the principal ports.

Climate – when to come

The climate is among the mildest in Britain, drier than the southwest and warmer than the east coast, with annual average temperature of 50°F (10°C). Sheltered by the

Lewes town centre

Come rain or shine

Downs, the coast is in the lee of cold north winds, and in winter the sea also helps keep the temperature above the national average. Resorts vie with each other over the amount of sun they have: Bognor Regis claims to have more hours of sunshine than anywhere else on Britain's mainland. Having said that, this is Britain, and the weather is known to be changeable: umbrellas are a sensible part of any luggage.

Come in April to see the bluebells in Slindon wood. Catch the orchids and other wild flowers on the south slopes of the Downs in June and July. The warmest months are July and August, with Adonis Blue butterflies and larks ascending. The sea should be temperate enough for swimming from mid-July to mid-September: it is always best after the tide has rolled in over sands heated up by the sun. Come in autumn to watch the seagulls chase the ploughmen and to see the birdlife in the wetlands of Amberley Wild Brooks, Pagham and Chichester Harbour and in the Cuckmere valley. Come for a winter weekend browsing the Brighton Lanes or sitting by a log fire in a country pub.

Spring blooms

A sheep-farming past

Industry and economy

The majority of employment around the South Downs is in the service sector, which was hit hard in the recession of the early 1990s. Unemployment is a problem and Brighton is enlivened by buskers and beggars.

The Downs have lost many of their sheep and most of its cattle, being left to the plough which furrows deeper and deeper. Vegetables are grown around Worthing and Selsey. Fewer than 4 percent of the population works in agriculture. There are no large industries in the area. Shoreham, the largest port between Dover and Portsmouth, imports cereals and oil, and Newhaven, the cross-Channel ferry port, has a commercial fishing fleet.

Reaping new benefits

Population

The population of Sussex is 1.25 million and around 75 percent live in the coastal conurbation which stretches unremittingly from Littlehampton to Seaford. Much of the housing is unattractive and poorly planned, following the post-World War I enthusiasm for 'homes for heroes' and the building booms in the 1930s and '50s, which produced so much suburban housing. In the 1970s and '80s the population growth in Sussex was the second largest of any English county.

Brighton New Agers

Traditionally, the typical Sussex character is a stubborn country person, slow to anger, reluctant to make speedy decisions, a person who 'will not be druv'. These were often the first yokels, Cold Comfort farmers, which city people encountered. They celebrated the seasons, smoked clay pipes, baked suet pies and believed in witches.

In his prime, the Sussex labourer wore a smock or 'round frock', which could be worn back to front when the front got dirty. These were the 'hog stoppers', smocks with enough material to hold out to catch a pig. But if the material might get in the way, when reaping, for example, a waist length 'ban-yan' could be worn. Linseed oil was rubbed into the material to make it waterproof and it seems to have been highly successful in keeping out the weather. A second frock, of good linen and embroidered on the collar, shoulders and cuffs, was kept for church and other important occasions, when a wide-awake or top hat would set it off.

Sussex folk were good drinkers, liked to sing songs, and had healthy children, many of whom were born out of wedlock, which the historian Arthur Beckett described as a pronounced feature in the social life of Sussex peasantry, due to the lack of entertainments and the proximity of the sexes. This was a feudal society, imposed by William

Joining in the community spirit

the Conqueror, who granted rights over the rapes to the noblemen who helped him win the Battle of Hastings: Roger de Montgomery in Chichester and Arundel, William de Braose in Bramber and William de Warenne in Lewes, all of whose families were around for some time.

Even today the owners of the great estates of Arundel, Cowdray, Goodwood, Petworth, Parham, Glynde, Firle, and Eastbourne, can trace their families back, if not to the Conqueror, then many hundreds of years.

Language

Sussex dialect disappeared along with the smock around the time of World War I, but some vestiges remain, and some words are worth recalling. A shepherd, who lived a hard life out on the Downs in all weathers, would count his sheep... 'one-erum, two-erum, cockerum, shu-erum, shitherum, shatherum, wineberry, wagtail, tarry-diddle, den.' A carter would call out to his horse, 'Muther wut,' when he wanted it to turn right.

Morris man

Local inhabitants referred to the Downs as The Hill, added an 'e' in plurals to make ghosts 'ghostes' and had no use for the aspirant h. In fact the word Down comes from the Saxon *dun*, meaning hill. Stane is probably from the Saxon *stan* (stone). Stane Street is the name given to the road the Romans built from Chichester to London, and its variants appear in The Steyne in Bognor and Worthing and in the Old and New Steine in Brighton. Steyning was the town of stone, as the suffix *-ing* denotes a settlement.

All place names are English: there are no Celtic names. The Saxons were brutal in their conquest. Pevensey (then called Anderida or Andred) was the last bastion of Romano-Britons and in 490AD, according to the *Anglo-Saxon Chronicle*, 'This year Aelle and Cissa beseiged the city of Andred and slew all that were therein.'

Other Sussex curiosities are 'twittens', passages between streets, as in Lewes, and 'catcreeps' in Brighton, steps between streets on different levels. You are unlikely these days to hear a diminutive person called a 'tibster', a no-good person an 'ibidioy', or someone slovenly called a 'rubishy-buster' or, with cross-Channel influence, 'deshabil'. But if someone tells you they are 'beazled' (weary), 'no-how' (poorly) or 'about as common' (as well as can be expected), or talk about their charrie (child), you will know they are real locals who wunt be druv.

Silly Sussex it has sometimes been called, and this may seem like a reference to some simple-minded folk. But there is a different etymology: *Silly Child* is an ancient Christmas carol, the word silly coming from the Saxon *selig*, which means holy or happy. The Downs are certainly a happy place to be.

French influences were imported by William the Conqueror

Historical Highlights

500,000BC Boxgrove Man, the first known man in Britain.

4000BC Farmers arrive in the region and land clearing begins.

3000BC Arrival of Neolithic peoples who create a camp fort at the Trundle and Long Barrow at Bevis's thumb and flint mine at Cissbury.

300–200BC Iron Age hill forts are built at the Trundle and Cissbury, the largest earthworks in Sussex. Hill forts such as Mount Caburn, Lewes, also built.

75BC Invasion of the Atrabate Belgic tribes under Commius, acting as envoy and advance party for the Romans. They settle around Chichester.

AD42 Roman invasion, aided by Cogidubnus, who ruled as king in Chichester.

AD50–100 Roman domestic building begins. Villas in Angmering, Arundel, Southwick and Fishbourne Palace (AD75). Stane Street built, from Chichester to London (AD70). Amphitheatre built in Chichester (AD90). Coastal defences with garrison forts overseen by the Count of the Saxon Shores.

400–410 Legions withdraw to defend Rome.

477–490 Saxons invade and establish kingdom of South Saxons. The last Roman-British slain at Pevensey and Saxon occupation complete.

681 St Wilfred lands at Selsey and converts Sussex to Christianity.

771 Offa of Mercia subjugates Sussex.

850–1000 Continual Danish raids along the coast. Alfred the Great of Wessex instigates building of fortifications in Chichester, Lewes and Pevensey.

960 Sompting Saxon church is built.

1064 Harold I prays at Bosham church before setting sail for Normandy, as illustrated in the Bayeaux tapestry.

1066 Saxon army is defeated by William of Normandy. William divides Sussex into six rapes, each with access to the sea, though their ports were often miles from the sea.

1086 Domesday survey puts the population of Sussex at around 10,000, and shows Brighton villagers paid 4,000 herrings a year to the local lord in rent.

1091 Building of Chichester Cathedral begins.

1246 Death of Richard of Wyke, bishop of Chichester, canonised 14 years later.

1264 Simon de Montfort and the barons defeat Henry III at Lewes, leading to the Mise of Lewes and the start of English parliamentary government.

1337–1448 Hundred Years' War: south coast ports are subjected to devastating raids by the French. Monastic buildings attached to French abbeys are dissolved, including Wilmington Priory (1414).

1347–50: The Black Death.

1539 Monasteries dissolved by Henry VIII, including Boxgrove, Lewes and Michelham.

1550–1600 The great Tudor manor houses built, including Cowdray House, Danny, Glynde, Parham and Winston.

1555–7 Seventeen Protestant Martyrs burnt at Lewes under Queen Mary.

1588 Beacons lit across South Downs to warn of the arrival of the Spanish Armada.

1622 First recorded game of cricket played in England, at Boxgrove Priory.

1642 Civil War. Sussex takes the Parliamentary side: the suburb of St Pancras, Chichester, destroyed in Parliamentary siege, and Arundel castle is damaged by siege a year later.

1651 Charles II hides in Brighton and escapes to France.

1712 Pallant House in Chichester is built.

1715–83 Lancelot (Capability) Brown, landscape gardener of Petworth House and Sheffield Park. Parks at Arundel, Goodwood and Cowdray follow his style.

1727 Halnacker Windmill built, the oldest tower windmill in Sussex.

1750 Dr Richard Russell of Lewes advocates sea water as a therapy and starts the seaside bathing vogue.

1768 Thomas Paine, author of *The Rights of Man*, takes up residence in Lewes.

1783 The Prince of Wales first visits Brighton.

1793 Cowdray House, the grandest Tudor manor in Sussex, is gutted by fire.

1804–10 A series of towers, known as Martello towers (47 in Sussex), are built along coast to counter threat of French Invasion.

1806 The Royal Crescent, the first domestic crescent, built in Brighton.

1807 Buttermarket is built in Chichester.

1809 The last iron forge, at Ashburnham, is closed.

1818 The building of the Royal Pavilion in Brighton is completed.

1825 Kemp Town inaugurated.

1830 Coastguard system and village policemen introduced to combat smuggling.

1832 Death of John Ellman of Glynde who developed the Southdown sheep.

1848 King Louis Philippe of France, escaping uprisings, arrives in Newhaven at the start of his exile.

1859 Coastal forts (Newhaven) built under further threat of invasion.

1863 Railway network established.

1897 Rudyard Kipling comes to live in Rottingdean.

1914–18 World War I. The Dome in Brighton is used as a hospital for the Indian army. Brighton Pier is later used as the setting for the 1969 film of *Oh! What a Lovely War*.

1934 Glyndebourne Opera House opens.

1936 Shoreham Airport is built.

1941 Virginia Woolf drowns herself in the River Ouse.

1939–45 World War II. Heavy bombing of ports and seaside towns. 3,000 bombs fall on Littlehampton, 4,000 on Eastbourne, which is evacuated. Petworth school bombed: 28 boys and two teachers are killed. Defences set up all along the coast and piers weakened to prevent enemy vehicles from landing. Residents are given 48 hours to evacuate Bungalow Town, Shoreham, which is completely destroyed for defensive purposes. Battle of Britain fought in 1940 over Southern England by fighter aircraft from airfields such as Tangmere and Ford.

1961 Fishbourne Roman Villa discovered.

1962 Festival Theatre, Chichester opens.

1972 South Downs Way is declared the first long-distance bridleway by the Countryside Commission.

1975 Brighton's West Pier closes.

1981 Brighton's naturist beach opens.

1989 Uppark is burned down..

1984 IRA bomb attempt on Margaret Thatcher and the Conservative cabinet in the Grand Hotel, Brighton.

1987 Hurricane winds devastate woodlands across South Downs, including Slindon, Chanctonbury and Stanmer Park.

1992 Chichester is flooded.

1993 Boxgrove Man discovered.

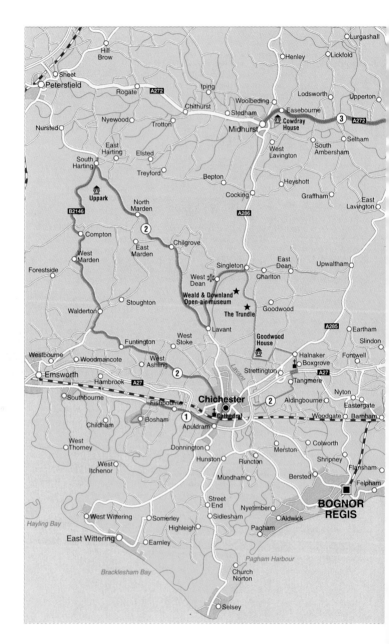

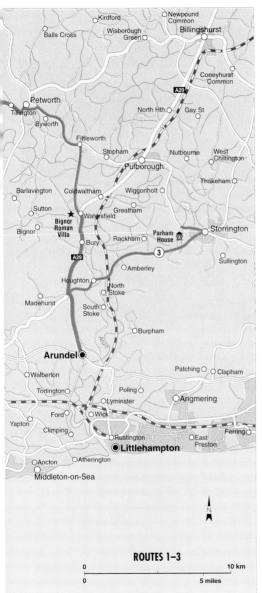

Chichester Cathedral, Route 1

15

Goodwood House, Route 2

Arundel Castle, Route 3

ROUTES 1–3

| 0 | 10 km |
| 0 | 5 miles |

Market Cross

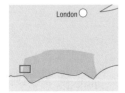

Route 1

Chichester and Surroundings

Chichester – Market Cross – Chichester District Museum – Pallant House – Cathedral – Fishbourne Roman Villa – Bosham (5 miles/8km) *See map, p14–15*

The cathedral city of Sussex is on the low level plain at the foot of the Downs, and the fingers of water which grope their way towards it provide the largest recreational stretch of navigable water on the south coast. This route takes in the Georgian city of Chichester, moves on to the Roman Palace at Fishbourne and ends at Bosham, Chichester Harbour's most attractive village, only 10 minutes away.

History

The coastal plain juts out to Selsey Bill on the Manhood Peninsula 10 miles (16km) south of Chichester, where in AD681 St Wilfred, a former bishop of York, brought Christianity to Sussex, and showed the fishermen how to use nets. Selsey, according to the Venerable Bede, derived from the name Seal's Island, and 'Manhood' is probably from the hundred of Mainwood. Wilfred built a cathedral at Selsey, but the see was moved to Chichester in the reorganisation of the kingdom under the Normans and the Selsey church sunk beneath eroding waves.

From Trundle to Chichester

Chichester had been founded by the Celtic Belgae who moved down from their encampment on the Trundle (*see page 22*) and taken over by the Romans, who named it Noviomagus, surrounded it with a flint wall and laid out the town as it is today. A mosaic floor from the Roman Forum can be seen in the cathedral which was built over it. The largest collection of Roman mosaics found in Britain

are nearby at Fishbourne, where a palace was uncovered in 1960. Uniquely, Chichester has had the same see and parishes since Saxon times.

Sights

There is no easier city than ★★★ **Chichester** (pop. 24,100) to find your way around. The old flint city walls draw a near perfect circle around it and four straight Roman streets – North Street, South Street, West Street and East Street – draw a cross through the middle. These radiate from the octagonal ★ **Market Cross**, built of Caen stone in 1501 to provide shelter for the poor.

East Street is the main shopping street, where livestock used to be driven in to market. The neoclassical **Corn Exchange** (1830) is on the right, and Little London, almost opposite, leads up to the **Chichester District Museum** (Tuesday to Saturday, 10am–5.30pm; admission free), which gives an account of the city and its trades.

Buttermarket

North Street leads up past the **Buttermarket** (1807), now a small shopping arcade, the Saxon church of **St Olave's**, now a religious bookshop, and the colonnaded **Council Chambers** (1731). Turn right here down Lion Street to St Martin's Square and the almshouses of **St Mary's Hospital**, founded in 1253. This still-functioning charity includes a large chapel which has been divided into small dormitories for its residents, who are summoned to prayer every morning by the chapel bell. There is no other almshouse like it left in the world, and visits can be arranged by telephoning the Matron (tel: 01243 783377 or 532516).

Part of the city wall

St Martin's square leads to **Priory Park** in the northeast corner of the city. This is the site of the Norman motte and bailey **castle** mound, and a good section of the city wall can be walked along here, giving views of the city (a leaflet describing the wall walks can be bought in the Tourist Office). Also in the park is the isolated **Guildhall**, long bereft of the 13th-century Franciscan priory to which it was attached. In 1804 the visionary poet William Blake was tried and acquitted of charges of High Treason in the building which now serves as a summertime gallery. On the far side of the walls is the **Festival Theatre** (*see Culture, page 63*), a highly successful modern venue with ticket sales running to half a million a year.

The **Tourist Office** is in South Street, which leads down to the station and the canal that connects to Chichester Harbour. On the east side of South Street is the Pallants, the finest Georgian part of town, exemplified in ★★ **Pallant House**, reached down West Pallant (10am–5.15pm, closed Sundays, Mondays, Bank Holidays; admission fee). Built in 1712 for Henry Peckham, a wine merchant, this carefully restored home has a number of original features. It

Pallant House

also contains an impressive, rotating art collection by mainly 20th-century British painters, including Graham Sutherland, Paul Nash and Ivon Hitchens. It is the amalgamation of three collections, inspired by works amassed by Walter Hussey, Dean of Chichester Cathedral from 1955–77, who, with Bishop Bell, was instrumental in giving modern British art a place in the cathedral. The Garden Gallery at the back, the original owner's kitchen, has regular exhibitions of other works.

West Street has the elegant facade of the Dolphin and Anchor, a coaching inn where General Eisenhower stayed the night before D-Day. Opposite is the ★★★ **Cathedral**, a light and graceful space that mixes Gothic with Romanesque and embraces bright modern art. Construction was begun in 1091 and the main Norman work was carried out under Bishop Luffa, who died in 1123. The cloisters, spire and bell tower were built in the early 15th century, though the spire disastrously collapsed in the 19th century, and massive restoration was carried out under Sir George Gilbert Scott (1811–78). Chichester is the only English cathedral with a separate campanile and the **bell tower**, with eight bells dating from 1583, is immediately visible: it has a souvenir shop in its ground floor.

Entrance to the cathedral is through the west portico. The **nave**, with geometric patterns on the architraves of the stout colonnade, is copied from the Abbaye aux Hommes, built for William the Conqueror in Caen in Normandy. To the left is the St Michael or **Sailor's Chapel** [A], to the right is the modern **font** [B] of polyphant stone (1983) by John Skelton. The **Bell-Arundel screen** [C] (1475) straight ahead shuts off the quire, which has well carved stalls from around 1330. The fine organ has Re-

Chichester Cathedral

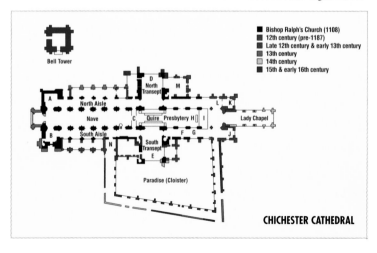

Bell Tower

■ Bishop Ralph's Church (1108)
■ 12th century (pre-1187)
■ Late 12th century & early 13th century
▨ 13th century
▢ 14th century
■ 15th & early 16th century

North Aisle

Nave

South Aisle

D
North Transept

M

C Quire Presbytery H □ I

Lady Chapel

L K

F G

J

South Transept
E

N

Paradise (Cloister)

CHICHESTER CATHEDRAL

natus Harris pipes from 1678 and is a sign of the cathedral's musical tradition, shared by Gustav Holst (1874–1934) whose **tomb** [D] is in the north transept.

The north transept has painted panels of the bishops of Chichester by Lambert Bernard, who worked under the patronage of Robert Sherburne, bishop from 1508 to 1536. During the Reformation, he sided with Henry VIII, and he can be seen with the king in one of the many **painted panels** [E] in the south transept which show the church's history. Sherburne greatly endowed the cathedral and he was rewarded by a suitably rich **monument** [G] in the south quire aisle.

Just before this monument are two magnificent ★ **Romanesque stone panels** [F] (c1125). These show Christ being greeted at Bethany by Mary and Martha and The Raising of Lazarus, which has a Christ of immeasurable sadness.

Romanesque panel

A modern highlight of the cathedral is undoubtedly the ★ **altar tapestry** [H] by John Piper (1966) on the Sherburne screen. In brilliant colours it shows the four gospels and the four elements and it greatly enriches the presbytery. Behind it is the companion **Anglo-German Tapestry** [I] by Ursula Benker-Schirmer (1985), which hangs above the shrine of St Richard, Bishop of Chichester from 1245–53, and the burial place of George Bell, bishop from 1929–58. The tapestry recognises Bell's commitment to modern art and his work for German refugees.

The Piper tapestry

Other modern works of art to note in the east chapels are Graham Sutherland's *Noli Mi Tangere* (1962) in the **Chapel of St Mary** [J], the reredos in the **Chapel of St John the Baptist** [K] by Patrick Procktor (1984) and the stained window designed by ★ **Marc Chagall** [L] (1978) illustrating Psalm 150: 'Let everything that has breath praise the Lord.'

The **treasury** [M], beside the north transept, has a modest collection of items and the **library** above contains many original volumes, including some from John Donne, and a 'Breeches Bible' of 1595 which attributes to Genesis iii: 7 the lines: 'They sewed figge-tree leaves together, and made themselves breeches.' St Richard's **porch** [N] was the original access to the **cloisters**, which lead to a number of buildings within the precinct, including Vicars' Close, St Richard's Walk and the gateway to the Bishop's Palace and gardens.

From Chichester, take the main A27 towards Portsmouth. Almost immediately, a sign at a roundabout indicates the A259 and ★★ **Fishbourne Roman Palace** (February, November and December 10am–4pm; March to July and September to October 10am–5pm; August 10am–6pm; closed 16 December to 12 February; admission fee). A mile down

Meander in the Roman Garden

this road a turning on the right leads to Fishbourne station and the excavations, set rather unromantically near a housing estate and school. This is the largest Roman domestic building found north of the Alps. It covered 5.6 acres (2.3ha), and it may have belonged to the Celtic client king Tiberius Claudius Cogidubnus. Begun around AD75, it burnt down some 200 years later. It had four wings, and the modern museum covers most of the north wing. Its 100 rooms all had mosaic tiled floors, a great feature of the site. In the grounds hedging plants follow the original pattern, and a **Roman Garden** has been planted with medicinal and culinary plants known to have been used at the time.

A boat in Bosham

Continue down the road a few minutes to ★★ **Bosham** (pronounced *Bozzum*, pop. 3,800), the most delightful village among the marshlands of Chichester harbour. Out of season park by the quay, but bear in mind the tide comes racing in to cover this road, and sometimes even laps at doorways, which accounts for their high steps. The Danish king Canute (994–1035) is said to have demonstrated his mortal inability to hold back the waves here and one of his daughters is thought to have been buried in the **Holy Trinity Church**, claimed to be the oldest site of Christianity in Sussex. The church's Saxon tower was a place of safety during raids and the Bayeaux Tapestry depicts King Harold leaving the church to meet William of Normandy.

Walk along the quay to the water mill, one of the best appointed yacht clubs in the country, and the **Raptackle**, a black barn on the jetty that once bulged with the ropes and gear of busy ships. A pint of ale in the Anchor Bleu, a snug pub which came to prominence in episodes of *The Saint* television series, is a fitting end to the visit.

The Raptackle

Route 2

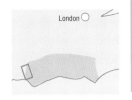

The West Sussex Downs

Tangmere – Boxgrove Priory – Goodwood – the Trundle hill fort – Singleton – West Dean Gardens – South Harting – Uppark (35miles/ 56 km) *See map, p 14–15*

This circular tour around the north of Chichester gives a flavour of the rural west Sussex Downs. Starting to the east of the city, it climbs above Goodwood racetrack to the Trundle, the Celtic capital of the region, with magnificent views across Chichester and its harbours to the Isle of Wight. The reconstruction of simple homes in the Weald and Downland Museum evokes rural Sussex, in contrast to the fine estate of Uppark. Finally, a rural ride through hamlets and sheep-grazed downlands leads back to the cathedral town.

Tangmere, 3 miles (5km) east of Chichester, operated as a fighter aerodrome from 1917 to 1970 and was one of the south of England's Battle of Britain airfields. The **Military Aviation Museum** (March to October 10am–5.30pm, February and November 10am–4.30pm; admission fee) in a former hanger plots the decisive air battles of 1940. Douglas Bader was its most famous flyer. H.E. Bates, author of *Fair Stood the Wind for France*, was stationed here, and undercover French resistance agents, trained at nearby Bignor Manor, were flown from here into occupied France. Among planes on display is a Hawker Hunter, the last aircraft to fly from the airfield.

Aerodrome at Tangmere

    Turning right into Tangmere village, the road leads back to the A27, crossing it towards Boxgrove. Ahead on a high point (415ft/127m) on the Downs is **Halnacker windmill**, pronounced Hanneker, the oldest tower mill in Sussex. Built it 1727, it fell into disuse in 1900, but was maintained as a landmark, as it can easily be spotted far out to sea.

Boxgrove, where archaeological digs in 1995 found Britain's earliest human, dating back 500,000 years, is known for its ★ **Priory**. Only the priory church survived the dissolution of the monasteries, though remains of an extended nave can be seen. Ruins of the cloister and conventual buildings lie to the north of the church, including a two-storey Prior's lodging and long grain barn in the grazing fields beyond. The Benedictine Order was established here in 1105 as a dependent of the Abbey of Lessay in Normandy. It may have employed the same architects as Chichester cathedral, and Lambert Barnard executed the ceiling paintings in the early 16th century. The church is dedicated to St Blaise, patron saint of wool-

Boxgrove Priory

combers, and it has a fine chancel and unusual transepts. In the chantry is an elegant early Renaissance tomb of the 9th Lord De La Warr.

From Boxgrove the road crosses the A285, which here follows the route of the Roman Stane Street which went from Chichester to London. Ahead are the seeming miles of 10ft-high (3m) flint wall that surrounds **Goodwood**, one of the great Sussex estates, which takes in a race course, a motor racing circuit, aerodrome, country park, golf course and hotel, not to mention countless acres of downland. One way of taking it all in is with a pleasure flight, organised by Goodwood Flying School at the aerodrome (tel: 01243 774656).

Goodwood House

The whole estate is now big business with a corporate air. Ancestral home of the Dukes of Richmond, it was acquired in 1729 by the first duke, Charles, the bastard son of Charles II and his French mistress, Louise de Querouaille. His grandson, the third duke, also Charles, extended a hunting lodge into ★ **Goodwood House** (open most Sunday and Monday afternoons, April to September, tel: 01243 774107). This flint turreted mansion at the heart of the estate was designed by James Wyatt (1746–1813) as an octagon, but only three sides were completed by 1790 when the duke ran out of money. The state rooms gleam with treasures, with paintings by Canaletto, Stubbs and Reynolds, with Sèvres porcelain, Gobelin tapestries and French furniture, much of it collected by the third duke when he was ambassador at the Versailles court of Louis XV.

All set for 'Glorious Goodwood'

The well-appointed and well planted **Country Park** surrounding the house adds majesty to the downland landscape. On the north side of the park is Goodwood's peerless **racecourse**, one of the world's great natural sporting venues, which basks in a natural amphitheatre with wide open views of the Downs. Each July 'Glorious Goodwood' becomes part of the fashionable season: 'A garden party with racing tacked on,' was how King Edward VII described it.

Trundle: Celtic capital

Just beyond the racecourse, as the road starts to descend again, is a car park for visitors to the ★★ **Trundle** on the summit a few minutes' walk away. This 12½-acre (5-hectare) Iron-Age fort with 17-ft (5-m) ramparts was built about 250BC on a 1,500-year-old neolithic causeway camp and forms three concentric rings, from which it derived its name: from the Saxon *tryndel* meaning circle. There were flint mines nearby and it was the Celtic capital of the region until 50BC when it was abandoned and the people moved down to Chichester.

The view from the Trundle is the best to be had on the west Sussex Downs, marred only by the communications mast at the top.

A few minutes beyond the Trundle is the ★★★ **Weald and Downland Open-air Museum** (1 March to 31 October 11am–5pm daily; 1 November to 28 February Wednesday, Saturday, Sunday 11am–4pm; 26 December to 2 January 11am–4pm; admission fee). More than three dozen timber-framed buildings from all over the Downs as well as the Weald of Sussex and Kent, dating back to the 13th century, have been brought to this 45-acre (18-hectare) site. They include shops and sheds, mills and barns, as well as domestic houses, and a farmhouse uprooted in the building of the Channel Tunnel.

In preserving these buildings many traditional crafts and skills have been employed, and some of them can be seen in action. There is an exhibition of woodland management, and a 16th-century farmstead has been landscaped to resemble the original. Shire horses, Sussex oxen and Southdown sheep are bred on the site.

The nearby village of **Singleton** is typical and attractive with flint houses and a good Saxon church. In 1915 the first Women's Institute in England was started here. **Charlton** and **East Dean** are similarly attractive small villages just to the east. The fame of the Charlton Hunt attracted the first Duke of Richmond to the area. Close by is **Chilsdown Vineyard** whose premises occupy a Victorian railway station (Monday to Saturday 10am–5.30pm, Sunday noon–5.30pm).

From Singleton, the A 286 continues to Midhurst (*see Route 3, page 25*). Turn back down the Lavant river valley toward Lavant to continue this round tour, past **West Dean Gardens** a 35-acre (14-hectare) garden with a dozen Victorian hot houses, a walled kitchen garden and a 2-mile (3.5-km) walk through an arboretum to the top of the Downs (daily 1 April to 31 October, 11am–5pm; admission fee). The gardens belonged to the extraordinary 20th-century art patron and eccentric Edward James, who had

Weald and Downland Open-air Museum

23

Singleton church

lobster-shaped telephones designed by Salvador Dali in his West Dean mansion (now a college specialising in crafts). James also donated the land for the Weald and Downland Museum.

A right turn just before the Lavant on the B2141 leads to South Harting. A pleasant drive, it meanders through the hamlets of **Chilgrove** and **North Marden**, where a simple Norman church stands beyond a farmyard, and nearby **Up Marden** where the 13th-century country church, unrestored by the Victorians, looks little more than a simple barn.

South Harting

Like the Mardens, there are North, East and West Hartings, all of which are typical of the small communities that scatter the Downs. Anthony Trollope (1815–82), the author who introduced pillar boxes to Britain, spent the last years of his life in **South Harting**, the most westerly village in Sussex. The naturalist Gilbert White (1720–93), who fancifully described the South Downs as 'mountains', also lived here.

Uppark

At the T-junction just before South Harting, signposts point left to ★★★ **Uppark** (National Trust; 1 June to 31 October, Sunday to Thursday 1–5.30pm; gardens and woodland walk open one hour earlier; admission fee and timed tickets). This magnificent 17th-century mansion, which has the appearance of a spoilt child's doll's house, was reopened in 1995, six years after being ravaged by a serious fire, which destroyed the original 18th-century wallpapers and fabrics. The restoration itself is a masterpiece: 4,000 dustbins full of rubble and debris were pieced together in the most meticulous restoration ever undertaken by the National Trust.

Brilliantly situated at the top of the Downs (350ft/ 106m), with wonderful views, Uppark was built for the first Lord Tankerville by William Talman in 1690, and remodelled in 1819 by Humphry Repton who added two flanking buildings, the stables and kitchen. There is a good art and decorative arts collection and a dining room table which was danced on by the captivating Emma Hart (who was later to become Lord Nelson's Lady Hamilton), who, aged 17, came to stay for a year with the reprobate Sir Harry Fetherstonhaugh. As her mobility continued upwards, his spiralled downwards until, aged 70, he married Uppark's head dairymaid.

There is a also a glimpse of life 'below stairs': H.G. Wells's mother was a housekeeper, and he recalls his boyhood here in his *Autobiography*.

From Uppark the B2146 drifts lazily back through the rolling arable downland and the hamlets of Compton and West Marden towards Chichester.

Route 3

Midhurst and the Rother Valley

Midhurst – Cowdray – Petworth – Bignor Roman Villa – Bury – Amberley – Parham – Arundel (35 miles/58km) *See map, p 14–15*

Midhurst

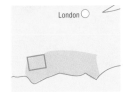

This route takes in the small but important market towns of West Sussex, the great country houses of Petworth and Parham, and Arundel, which has the finest castle in Sussex.

Midhurst *(see below)* is a quaint, red-tiled market town which makes a good base for touring the pretty little villages in the Rother valley and the surrounding Downs. On the north side of the town in open country beside the River Rother are the gaunt remains of ★ **Cowdray House** in **Cowdray Park**, one of Britain's best known polo grounds. The Tudor mansion was begun in 1492 by the son-in-law of the last of the de Bohun family who had been the local gentry. In 1793, it all but burnt down, and it has not been touched since.

Cowdray House and Park

On the other side of the road is **Easeborne**, the original town in which Midhurst parish lay. There was an Augustinian priory here and its surviving church contains the memorials to the Montague family who gained the estate, including Cowdray House, by marriage and had been cursed to perish by fire and water by the last monk they kicked out of Battle Abbey (just after the house burnt down, Viscount Montague was drowned in Switzerland, and his two heirs drowned at Bognor).

In ★ ★ **Midhurst** the 15th-century parish church is opposite Market Hall and Town Hall in **Market Square**, near the fine 15th-century half-timbered Eagle Inn where the Pilgrim Fathers stopped on the way to Southampton. Mar-

Petworth House and town

In Petworth's deer park

Amberley Museum

ket Square was the centre of the settlement that grew up outside the gates of the original de Bohan **Castle**, at the top of St Anne's Hill. The foundations of the encircling wall and buildings of this fortified manor house lie in a chestnut copse, which has good views over Cowdray Park.

To the east of Midhurst is **Petworth**, a town of myriad antique shops overshadowed by the great grey wall of ★★ **Petworth House** (National Trust; 1 April to 31 October daily except Monday and Friday, 1–5pm; admission fee), which lies in a 700-acre (280-hectare) deer park landscaped by Capability Brown (1715–83) and famously painted by J.M.W. Turner (1775–1851). The house, home to the Percy family since 1150, is a solid three-storey 17th-century slab containing the National Trust's largest art collection with paintings by Van Dyck, Lely, Gainsborough, Claud, Reynolds and Blake as well as Turner. Grindling Gibbons (1648–1721) executed some of his finest carvings here.

Petworth is a small town, which likes to call itself the centre for antiques in the south of England. Its shops sell quality items and Americans arrive by the coach load in summer to ship them away. There are few other distractions in the town. **The Doll House Museum** in the car park has a variety of scaled-down buildings inhabited by 2,000 tiny people (March to end October, Thursday to Sunday 10.30m–5.30pm; January and February, Sundays only 11.30am–4.30pm; admission fee). The **Cottage Museum** in Rosemary Lane is a reconstructed Victorian interior.

From Petworth, the A283 heads east towards **Fittleworth**. Just before the village a right turn is signposted to ★ **Bignor Roman Villa**, a route which passes the excellent Swan Inn, briefly touches the A29, then turns right again opposite **Bury**, where the writer John Galsworthy (1867–1933) lived at the end of his life. In the heart of expansive Downland fields the excavations are housed in little thatched buildings (March to May and October 10am–5pm, closed Mondays: June to September 10am–6pm; admission fee). The site dates from the first century AD and covers 4½ acres (1.8hectares) with a central courtyard. There are some fine mosaics depicting gladiators, Venus and Medusa.

Back on the main A29 the road goes up Bury Hill giving spectacular views down over the River Arun. From the roundabout the road drops down again towards Amberley Station, the entrance to the popular and successful ★ **Amberley Museum** (March 22 to October 29, Wednesday to Sunday, 10am–5pm; daily during local school holidays.) This 36-acre (15-hectare) site is centred on giant chalk pits, and it is principally an open-air industrial museum. Attractions include a narrow gauge railway, once used in the quarry, lime kilns, a brickmaking works and a blacksmith's forge.

Amberley itself, just beyond, is one of the most delightful villages in Sussex. Its thatched, flint houses are mellow and robust, its lanes leading from castle ruins to the Wild Brooks, the water meadows of the River Arun, are a picture of peace. The castle was built as a palace for the bishops of Chichester. Bishop Luffa, who did so much in the building of Chichester cathedral, is thought to have been responsible for the Norman chancel arch. The Tudor manor house was built by Bishop Sherburne.

Still waters: the River Arun

From Amberley the road leads to Storrington, and a left turn on entering the town turns back up to the entrance of ★★ **Parham House**, one of the finest Elizabethan mansions in England (Easter to first Sunday in October, Wednesday, Thursday, Sunday and Bank Holidays, gardens 1–6pm, house 2–6pm, last entry 5pm; admission fee). A corruption of 'pear homestead', it was originally a farm supplying Westminster Abbey. The E-shaped house was built in 1577 and has wonderful gardens which include a 4-acre (1.6-hectare) walled garden, orchard, maze and heronry.

27

Return to Amberley and the roundabout at the top of Bury Hill where the next exit leads to **Arundel** (pop. 3,000), passing the **cricket ground** on the left just before entering the town. Arundel is the seat of the Duke of Norfolk, England's Premier Duke and Earl Marshall of England, who is responsible for organising all royal ceremonial occasions, such as coronations, weddings and funerals. Touring cricket teams play the Duke of Norfolk's XI on the Arundel ground prior to a Test series in England.

Out and about in Arundel

The Norfolks are also one of the leading Roman Catholic families in England, and the neo-Gothic **cathedral** just past the cricket grounds on the right was built in 1870 by J.A. Hansome (1803–82), of Hansome Cab fame. It is well appointed and can be seen for miles around, though its interior is dull. On Corpus Christi, however, it is brightened with a flower carpet of around 30,000 blooms. Until it was built, the ducal family of Fitzalans used a chapel in the local 14th-century parish church opposite the castle. After a dispute in the 19th century this half of the church was sealed off and since then the only way to reach it has been through the castle, though it can now be seen through a glass partition from the Anglican half of the church, and still functions perfectly well.

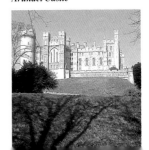
Arundel Castle

★★★ **Arundel castle** (2 April to last Friday in October, 12 noon–5pm, closed Saturdays and Good Friday; admission fee) is one of England's finest, set proud on the edge of the Downs as they drop away to the River Arun. It was built on the site of a Saxon fort in 1070 by Roger de Montgomery who is commemorated in the surviving

Wildfowl and Wetlands Centre

keep known as Montgomery's Tower. It was half demolished in a defence against Parliamentary forces in the Civil War and the flourish of turrets and chimney stacks is largely 19th-century. The interior is as stately and grand as a castle should be, with a huge Barons' Hall, Stone Hall, Grand Staircase and well-furnished dining and drawing rooms. Laurence and Lely are among the artists who painted generations of Norfolks in the picture gallery. Scenes in *The Madness of King George* were filmed here.

Behind the castle, parklands extend for 1,200 acres (480 hectares) and include **Swanbourne Lake**, with rowing boats. Just beyond, on the opposite side of the road, is the ★ **Wildflowl and Wetlands Centre** (9.30am–5.30pm in summer, 9.30am–4.30pm in winter, last admission one hour before closing; admission fee). There are ducks, geese and swans from all over the world, and the walk, via seven hides, is brightened by dragonflies, butterflies and the songs of reed warblers. Beyond the reserve is the Black Rabbit pub, ideally set by the river and the finishing point of an annual raft race from the bridge.

Arundel was a port mentioned in the Domesday Book and active up until the 19th century, with a quay, fish market and customs house. The ruins of a Blackfriars monastery are visible by the bridge, which leads up the steep High Street, with the **Tourist Information Office** and small **Museum and Heritage Centre** on the left (Easter to May and October, weekends and Bank Holidays; May to September daily 11am–5pm, Sundays 2–5pm, admission fee). A further small diversion is the **Toy and Military Museum**, the military being toy soldiers (Open daily Easter to October and on weekends in winter; admission fee.) Finally, Arundel is a good place for tea. Tarrant Street, just before the Tourist Office on the left of the High Street, has a choice of tea shops.

Route 4

Bognor to Shoreham

Bognor – Litttlehampton – Goring – Worthing– St Mary's, Sompting – Shoreham Airport – Lancing College Chapel (25 miles/40km) *See map, p30–1*

The south coast resorts from Bognor to Brighton are a former generation's playground which has been infilled by ribbon developments, with villas from the 1930s and '50s, and redbrick estates of more recent years. These popular Regency and Victorian resorts are entering the 21st century with theme parks and adventure playgrounds. But the Downs are still close by, and no amount of development can detract from this stretch of coast's best asset: its fine sandy beaches. Stretching between the mudflats and nature reserve of Pagham on the edge of Chichester harbour in the west to the mouth of the River Adur in the east, they have delighted summer crowds for a century. They also proved ideal for aircraft pioneers at Shoreham, while in Felpham, east of Bognor Regis, they produced a vision of the prophet Job for the poet John Milton (1608–74).

On the sunny south coast

29

Water slide at Butlin's South Coast World

Bognor Regis (pop 37,000) claims to be the sunniest place on the south coast. George V (1865–1936) bestowed the title of Regis on the town that his grandmother, Queen Victoria, had described as 'Dear little Bognor'. However, the ailing king, reportedly in response to the idea that he might soon be well enough to visit the resort, replied, 'Bugger Bognor' and expired.

The Regency town was championed by Sir Richard Hotham, a hatter from Southwark, who in 1787 began work on what he hoped to be a classy 'garden town' he endeavoured to have renamed Hothampton. He built Hotham House and gardens, now a park with boating lake and overshadowed by Butlin's South Coast World. The end of the pier fell into the sea in the 1960s, but the remaining jetty has provided a launching pad for 'Birdman' competitions to see how far man, unassisted, can fly.

Bailiffscourt

Eight miles (12km) east the River Arun reaches the sea at **Littlehampton** (pop 22,000), where the tide rushes in and out of the river mouth with great speed. There is a lifeboat station here, which has an open day in May. On the west side of the river are the wild sand dunes of ★ **Climping beach**. Climping village is on the north side of the A259, and its church, St Mary's, has some fine Norman decoration. Near the beach is Bailiffscourt, a handsome hotel and restaurant, which looks ancient but was entirely constructed on this site in the 1930s. Littlehampton's beach is a vast flat stretch of firm sand, and its main seafront entertainment is Harbour Park, billed as a 'New England fishing village' but really a glorified funfair (Easter to September, weekends and Whitsun; daily July and August). There is a small **museum** in the town (Tuesday to Saturday, 10.30am–4.30pm; admission free), but a more novel entertainment is to take a tour of **The Body Shop**, which has its headquarters in Littlehampton. This shows the preparation of the 'green' company's products (telephone first: 01903 731500).

East of Littlehampton the coast road turns inland at **Rustington** and goes through the unbroken urbanisations of **East Preston**, **Ferring** and **Goring**, where it is easier to get back to the sea. An oddity in Goring is the **English Martyrs Church**, a 1968 building attached to the original 18th-century church, with a replica of the Sistine Chapel's ceiling by Gary Bevans.

Goring's 'Sistine ceiling'

On the north side of Goring is **Highdown Chalk Gardens** (weekdays 10am–4.30pm, weekends 10am–8pm; closed at weekends between October and March), an exercise in what can possibly grow in an old chalk pit, and nearby the 269-ft (83-metre) **Highdown Hill**, a hill fort and cemetery site dating from the New Stone Age. The naturalist Richard Jeffries (1848–87) spent his last years at Goring. He is buried in the cemetery at **Broadwater**, as is the writer W.H. Hudson (1841–1922) who stayed for a while in the same house Jeffries occupied.

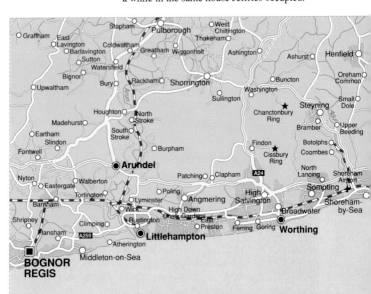

Broadwater, which has a Norman church, was the original settlement from which Worthing (pop 95,000, the largest town in West Sussex) grew. It has now engulfed Broadwater, Durrington, Goring and Sompting and the old village of **Tarring**, where there was an episcopal palace in the 14th century. **Sompting** has been dissected by the A27, leaving its fine ★ **Saxon church** away from developments. This merits a detour. Dating from AD960, it is one of only a handful of Saxon churches in the country, and it is the only one with a Rhenish Helm roof, made with oak shingles, a style borrowed from the Rhineland in Germany. The timbers inside the tower are more than 1,000 years old. The rest of the slate-roofed church was rebuilt by the Normans. Note the hassocks embroidered with views of the Downs and the sea by the faithful parishioners.

Sompting's Saxon church

★★ **Worthing** is a tidy town with some fine houses and elegant terraces. Entertainment is provided on the **pier**, which has a nightclub at the end, and the **Lido** on the promenade (weekends from mid-March, daily from Whitsun to October 31). More sedate is **Beach House Park**, well maintained gardens where the national bowls championships take place. Sedateness is still the order of the day in this town which gave its name to John Worthing in *The Importance of Being Earnest*, which Oscar Wilde wrote during a stay here. This association with Wilde has inspired an annual festival named after him, and there is no shortage of other entertainments, from tea dances to classical music and popular shows.

In Beach House Park

ROUTES 4 & 6

0   10 km

0   5 miles

A history of costume, trades and the locality going back to early man, is shown in the **Museum and Art Gallery** (April to September 10am–6pm, October to March 10am–5pm, closed Sundays, admission free) in Chapel Road, next to the Assembly Halls, Library and Tourist Information Office.

The A259 to Brighton takes off along the coast to **Shoreham-by-Sea** on the mouth of the River Adur. At the roundabout just before the bridge that crosses the Adur, a signpost points to ★★ **Shoreham Airport**. This is an historic airfield, one of the first in Britain, and the wonderful 1936 Art Deco **Terminal Building** evokes the excitement of early flying days. Helicopter and aeroplane joy rides are offered by a number of companies operating in the airfield, and the Terminal Building is a grand place for a snack or a drink while watching the activity on the tarmac.

SHOREHAM AIRPORT

32

The River Adur divides East and West Sussex and creates Shoreham's harbour and the busy neighbouring quays of Portslade-by Sea. As a shipper of slag, scrap metal and aggregates Shoreham has a gritty feel, but it has always been active. The town is made up of Old Shoreham and New Shoreham, the latter created in 1200 when the sea receded from the former. In its heyday 146 years later, the port provided Edward III with 26 ships and 329 men for an invasion of France. King John landed here to claim the throne on the death of his brother Richard, and Charles II made his hasty escape to France through the port.

There are few signs left of the flourishing old port, but there is a fine little 14th-century flint building, **Marlipins**, built of chequered black flint and white Caen stone, and with a single 40-ft (12-m) beam supporting the upper storey. It now houses the **Museum of Local and Maritime History** (May to September, Tuesday to Saturday 10am–1pm, 2–4.30pm, Sundays 2–4.30pm; admission fee). Shoreham has two good churches: St Nicholas and St Mary de Haura.

Shoreham Beach was known as Bungalow Town until World War II, when Field Marshall Montgomery, in charge of sea defences, gave its residents 48 hours to evacuate the community before completely destroying it. The shore provided two benefits earlier in the 20th century. It had a successful silent-film studio, which made such cinematic hits as *Little Dorritt*, and it was used as a landing strip by early aviators.

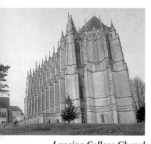

Lancing College Chapel

Behind the airport are the humps of the South Downs and the neo-Gothic **Lancing College Chapel** (Monday to Saturday 10am–4pm, Sunday noon–4pm, plus all services) with an interior nave 745ft (227m) in height. The public school was founded in 1848, and the chapel is a landmark.

Route 5

Brighton beach

Brighton

Toy Museum – North Laine – Royal Pavilion – Brighton Museum and Art Gallery – The Lanes– Fishermen's Museum – Palace Pier – Sea Life Centre – Volks Railway – Marina

33

'Nobody can be altogether good in Brighton and that is the great charm of it.' Richard Jeffries (1848–87) summed up the raffish air of the south coast's premier resort, where the Prince Regent set the pace with a secret and illegal marriage, and its hotels became synonymous with 'dirty weekends', though these days the spectacular Royal Pavilion is proving a popular venue for legitimate, civil weddings. A university town and the largest in Sussex (pop 150,000), Brighton tumbles over big-dipper roads across the Downs to arrive at a 7-mile (4.5-km) seafront, smothering smart Hove to the west, and Kemp Town to the east and pointing two fingers – fun Palace Pier and the beleaguered West Pier – at the sea. A centre for the antiques trade, its lanes, twittens and catcreeps are a browser's delight and there are probably more inexpensive restaurants per square mile here than anywhere else in Britain.

Beside the seaside

History

A Saxon gave his name to the town. He was Brighthelm and he settled in the Pool valley. Brighthelmston was the name the settlement was known by up until the 19th century. It grew up in the neat square bordered today by North, West, East streets and the sea. Fishermen lived on the coast, and farmers lived in the slightly higher land. In the middle of the square, fields of hemp were grown to supply the fishermen with their nets. These hemp shares were crossed with paths known as lanes, from which the famous Lanes derive their name. Historians give The North Laine a different etymology: the land on the north side of the Lanes was divided into leased pasture and arable fields called 'laines' *(see page 6)*.

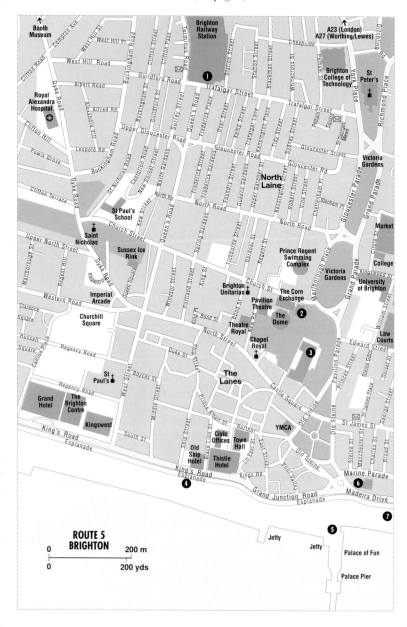

ROUTE 5
BRIGHTON

0 ————— 200 m

0 ————— 200 yds

By the end of the 16th century, this unprepossessing settlement, which had been torched by the French in the Hundred Years' War, supported 400 fishermen with 80 boats and 10,000 nets.

Visitors began arriving in the 18th century when the road from London still went via Newhaven. In 1750 Dr Richard Russell of Lewes pronounced in a tract the efficacy of sea water, both to drink and to bathe in, and the flood gates opened. Twenty-five years later, Brighton had become London-on-Sea, a favourite haunt of Prinny, the Prince of Wales, who in 1784 drove a coach from London along the new, direct road in 4 hours and 30 minutes. His Royal Pavilion was completed by 1818 and a dozen years later the population was 40,000, and there were regular steamship crossings to Dieppe in France – a link which remains with Dieppe marketeers setting up their stalls in Brighton today. The Chain Pier, built as a jetty for the steamers, was replaced by the Palace Pier in 1899.

'Prinny'

Brighton's popularity has remained all this century, untarnished by its villains made famous in Graham Greene's *Brighton Rock*. It thrives as a weekend resort for the capital, and a conference centre for the major political parties, surviving the IRA bomb at the Conservative Party conference in 1984, which demolished a chunk of the prestigious Grand Hotel. Among current projects are fundraising plans to restore the Grade I listed West Pier, which has been closed since 1975.

The celebrated Palace Pier

35

Sights

Brighton Station is in the centre of town, and its large car park is the venue for a giant flea market every Sunday from 9am to 2pm. The station is at the top of Queen's Road, approached from below along Trafalgar Street where four of the bridge's arches are occupied by **The Sussex Toy and Model Museum** ❶ (10am–5pm; Sundays and Bank Holidays 11am–5pm; closed for lunch 1–2pm; entrance fee). Centred on a 1930s railway layout, it has a full collection of memorabilia for adults, with Arkitex, Bayko, Meccano and Lott's Tudor building sets, Triang and Dinky Toys, dolls, games and puzzles.

In Trafalgar Street, a kite shop provides a further excuse to get up on the Downs, and there may be some bargains in the pawnbrokers. This street leads down to **St Peter's**, Brighton's parish church, built in 1828 by Sir Charles Barry (1795–1860), architect of the Houses of Parliament in London. Trafalgar Street is the northern extremity of the **North Laine**, the centre of 'alternative' Brighton, which extends down Sydney Street, Kensington Gardens, Gardner Street and Bond Street to North Street. It was developed in the early 19th century as an area of low-cost housing and light industry. Its hippie air

Bargain hunt in the North Laine

A young scene

is reinforced by numerous antique and junk shops, by Merlin's Cave, Greenwich Village, Neal's Yard Remedies, and Revamps, which sells 1960s and '70s clothes, by jugglers' suppliers, vegan stockists, cheese specialists and vegetarian shoe-makers, by importers of merchandise from Latin America, Africa, India and Java, and by Brighton Peace Centre, representing a number of pressure groups. Kensington Coffee Shop, which has an upstairs terrace overlooking Kensington Gardens, is a lively meeting spot, and the whole area is buzzing on Saturday mornings when the antique market opens up with stalls along Upper Gardner Street.

Royal Pavilion

On the southeast side of the North Laine, between Church Street and North Street, is the ★★★ **Royal Pavilion** , the town's most celebrated landmark (June to September, 10am–6pm; October to March, 10am–5pm; closed December 25–26; admission fee). Built for the Prince Regent (George IV, 1820–30) by Henry Holland (1745–1806) and John Nash (1752–1835), it was begun in 1787 and completed in 1822, evidently inspired by the architecture of Mughal India.

The Prince Regent had originally rented a modest farm on this site when he was pursuing an affair with the Catholic Mrs Maria Fitzherbert who, even after they were secretly married, lived in a house built for her in 1804 in Old Steine, now the YMCA.

The Indian styling of the Pavilion was begun by the architect William Porden (1775–1822), who built the octagonal **Royal Stables** (1808) with a soaring dome, 80ft (24m) in diameter and 65ft (19m) tall, which is now the Dome Theatre. As a result of this, the Prince Regent brought in Nash to embellish Henry Holland's original design, which he did to great effect, adding onion domes and minarets. An underground passage eventually connected the two buildings.

George IV's niece, Queen Victoria, was not enamoured with the place, and she deserted it, taking the furniture and fittings with her and selling it, in 1850, to Brighton council. Recent restoration, however, has brought the building brilliantly back to life, and furniture has been returned, on loan from HM the Queen. Every room in the interior is exquisitely decorated with the bright oriental colours

BRIGHTON PAVILION

Nash's Eastern promise

and motifs fashionable at the time, and there are some fine coloured windows and skylights that suffuse it all with enormous cheerfulness. The interiors were designed by Frederick Grace (1779–1859) and Robert Jones. On the ground floor is the opulent **Banqueting Room**, laid and ready for a feast, with chinoiserie panels and a splendid gold dragon beneath burnished palm leaves holding the chandelier. Beyond is the **Great Kitchen**, befitting the food and drink-loving royal. As big as a ballroom with palm-tree shaped pillars, a 'modern' spit, and 500 copper pieces in the *batterie de cuisine*, it was a wonder of its time. **The Music Room** is also stunning, and a chance to hear a concert performance should not be missed.

37

Great Kitchen in its heyday

The first-floor apartments include Queen Victoria's four-poster with no fewer than six mattresses of feathers, horse hair and straw. Near a wonderfully satirical painting of *The Prince Regent Awakening the Spirit of Brighton* by Rex Whistler (1944), is The Queen Adelaide Tea Room which serves refreshments.

Queen Adelaide was the wife of William IV (1830–37), George IV's brother and successor. The **North Gate** on the estate is named after him and the adjoining building, in Church Street, ★★ **Brighton Museum and Art Gallery** ❸ (10am–5pm; 2–5pm on Sundays, closed Wednesdays; admission free), was built in 1873 on a site earmarked for Queen Adelaide's tennis courts. The museum has an excellent, eclectic collection, which has local interest, including Brighton's last cork shop from the North Laine, and an imaginative costume collection. It also has some fine Victorian paintings, and an extensive collection of Art Deco furniture and artifacts.

Museum piece

The **South Gate**, near the entrance to the Pavilion, was a gift from the people of India after the Pavilion had been used for a hospital for the Indian Army during World

Beached in the gardens

War I. The Chattri Indian War Memorial is on the Downs above Patcham. The **gardens** have been restored to John Nash's design, though the former ice house, which kept the kitchen food fresh, has not been rebuilt. It was on the edge of the garden in New Road opposite the colonnaded **Theatre Royal** (1806).

Below North Street are the **Lanes**, the heart of the old fishing town, where the more upmarket jewellers and antique shops huddle, as well as some of the busiest restaurants and most popular pubs, such as the Bath Arms, the Cricketers and the Derrek Carver, named after one of the Protestant martyrs burnt at Lewes in 1555 who owned a brewery that once stood here. Among other premises to look out for here are Pecksmiths perfume shop, the fortune teller Eva Petrulengro, and The Mock Turtle tea shop in Pool Valley.

To the south of the Lanes is Bartholomew Square, site of a monastic farm, where the **Town Hall** (1832) and **Tourist Information Centre** are. On the west side of the Lanes is Churchill Square and Western Road, the main modern shopping centre of town where the large chain stores occupy mostly 1930s buildings. From here Dyke Road leads past the church of **St Nicholas**, over-restored in the 19th century and dating from the 14th century, with a good 12th-century font, possibly from Lewes Priory. A number of colourful characters are buried in the churchyard including beach personalities Captain Nicholas Tattersall, who used to carry the naked Prince Regent into the sea, and Martha Gunn, the best known 'dipper'. Further up Dyke Road is the **Booth Museum** (10am–5pm, Sundays 2–5pm, closed Thursdays, Good Friday; admission fee), a natural history museum based on a 19th-century collection of stuffed birds.

Lunching in The Lanes

On the **seafront** just beyond the Lanes are the modern entertainment complex, The Brighton Centre, and the old hotels, the Grand and The Old Ship Hotel from where an annual dash to France commemorates Charles II's escape. Under an arch on the beach below the hotel is **Brighton Fishing Museum** ❹ (daily, admission free), which is a little bigger than the clinkerbuilt fishing 'punt' berthed inside it.

On Palace Pier

★★ **Palace Pier** ❺ is, of course, essential viewing. It's free, so are its deckchairs, and the entertainment is in strolling up and down. Attractions include an amusement arcade that roars to the sound of racing cars, weapons of unspeakable deadliness and small children trying to whack Crabby Crab. A funfair is at the end of the 1,700-ft (500-m) structure, and there two pubs, a karaoke bar and fish and chip restaurant.

The **Sea Life Centre** ❻ (daily, from 10am–6pm, 9am–7pm in summer; admission fee) is in the aquarium by the pier. Though this has modern underwater tunnels for close-up views of British sharks and stingrays, the aquarium has been here since Victorian times and some of the old displays remain.

Volk's Railway

The aquarium is on the corner of Madeira Drive, from where the little **Volk's Railway** ❼, the oldest electric railway in the country (built in 1883) runs for 1¼ miles (2km) along the sea front, stopping at Peter Pan's Playground and passing the nudist beach. Madeira Drive is where old crocks from the annual London to Brighton Vintage Car Runs and Cycle Rides end. Marine Drive, above it, leads to **Brighton Marina**, the largest in Europe, covering 77 acres (31 hectares) and providing berths for 2,000 boats. Shops and boutiques have been built in the Marina Village, and there is a cinema and large Asda supermarket, but it has yet to acquire the real character of Brighton.

Two other attractions just outside the centre of Brighton are worth seeing on a longer visit. The first, **Preston Manor** next to Preston Park in London Road, is an elegant Edwardian manor which evokes life above and below stairs (2 miles/3km north of Brighton, train to Preston park; 10am–5pm; Sundays 2–5pm; Mondays 1–5pm; admission fee.)

British Engineerium

The second, **The British Engineerium** in a Victorian pumping station in Nevill Road, Hove, has a collection of engines which get steamed up on the first Sunday of the month and on Bank Holidays (daily, 10am–5pm, admission fee). It is also worth looking out for current exhibitions at the **Hove Museum and Art Gallery** in New Church Road, Hove (Tuesday to Friday 10am–5pm, Saturday 10am–4.30pm, Sunday 2–5pm, closed Monday, admission free).

Chanctonbury

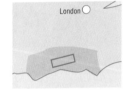

London ○

THE NATIONAL TRUST

CISSBURY RING

Cissbury

Route 6

The Central Downs

Cissbury Ring – Findon – Storrington – Chanctonbury Ring – Steyning – Bramber Castle – St Mary's House – Fulking – Devil's Dyke – Ditchling (32 miles/52km) *See map, p 30–1*

This route takes in the high spots of the central Downs at the back of Brighton, reaching the hill forts of Cissbury and Chanctonbury and Ditchling Beacon, all with great views over the coast. Starting near Worthing, it ends at Lewes (Route 7), and includes the pretty town of Steyning, which makes a good base for exploring this area.

There are two ways of getting to ★★★ **Cissbury Ring**. A signpost on the A24 north of Worthing directs visitors to the two main car parks, but if there are not many visitors, it is possible to drive closer to the 602-ft (183-m) summit by going through the village of **Findon**. This is race-horse country and every September for 700 years a sheep fair has been held in the village. At its central crossroads is the Village Hotel, a pub with a restaurant and a wide choice of beers, and Parhams, a butchers which sells meat and produce from its own farm. The road beside it leads to Cissbury Ring, and only the last few hundred yards need to be walked.

One of a chain of hill forts, Cissbury is named after the Saxon leader Cissa, but the hill fort was built here long before him, in 250BC. It covers 60 acres (24 hectares), and is the second largest in the country after Maiden Castle in Dorset. For the ramparts, a wooden wall was constructed to contain 60,000 tons of chalk excavated from the ditch. The site had already been occupied for around 4,000 years when some 300 flint mine shafts were dug, to a depth of up to 40ft (12m), using deer antlers as pick axes. The thick grass is springy underfoot: because the land here has never been ploughed, the rich and ancient fauna contains around 30 kinds of plants including eight orchids and the field fleawort used in bedding to combat the enemies of repose.

To reach ★★ **Chanctonbury Ring**, continue north on the A24, turning right at Washington. A mile further on, opposite the turning to Buncton, is a right turn up to Chanctonbury. A car park towards the end of the lane is a 20-minute hike short of the beech-planted 782-ft (238-m) summit, a walk that can be sticky when wet.

The plateau site is privately owned by the local Goring family. In 1760 Charles Goring, then a boy, planted the distinctive beech grove, a spiky wig which marks the site, though it took a battering in the 1987 storms. Ancient flint mines and burial grounds, an Iron Age hill fort and a Roman temple are all woven into Chanctonbury's past. So, too, are demonology and witchcraft, and a number of sightings and strange occurrences have been claimed. The devil may be evoked by running seven times round the ring on a moonless night.

Another way up to Chanctonbury is the pleasant 3-km (2-mile) footpath walk from ★★ **Steyning** (pronounced Stenning), a pleasing small town with 61 listed buildings. The church of **St Andrew** gives an idea of the importance of this town that once stood on a navigable river. Built by the Abbey of Fécamp in Normandy, to whom the estate was given by Edward the Confessor (1042–66), it has the most impressive Norman nave of any church in Sussex. It is approached through a heavy wood door, which still has its Norman hinges and sanctuary rings to which the hounded could cling to claim refuge. Inside are solid Norman, Caen-stone pillars with decorated arches and a stunning 38-ft (12-m) chancel arch. The church is dedicated to St Andrew though St Cuthman is thought to have been buried here, as well as Ethelwulf, father of Alfred the Great, in AD858. Opposite the church is the modern library and local **museum** (10.30am–12.30pm, 2.30–4pm, closed Thursday and Sunday).

Steyning town centre: Market House and hostelry

All the houses between the church and the High Street are worth examining, particularly the handsome half-timbered grammar school (1614). There are also a number of fine houses in High Street, including Market House, with a clock tower, which allows entrance into Cobblestone Walk, a courtyard of shops that lives in a time warp.

In Saxon times Steyning had its own mint, but the river which spread through marshland and brought prosperity

Bramber Castle

Springtime in Fulking

Jack and Jill windmills

through Cuthman's Port, became silted up, though not completely until the 19th century. Neighbouring **Bramber** suffered the same fate, and became a Rotten Borough, with 35 inhabitants returning a member of parliament. **Bramber Castle** (English Heritage) is little more than a few ruins of flint walls, including a 90-ft (27-m) tower, but it has the feeling of a mighty place. This was the fiefdom of William de Braose, who came over with the Conqueror, and it was the stronghold of the Rape. Ships used to tie up at a wharf alongside ★ **St Mary's House** (1470) in the High Street, which has a fine interior (Easter Sunday to September 30, Sunday and Monday, 2–6pm; Monday, Wednesday and Thursday in August 2–6pm. Admission charge).

From Bramber the road east follows the Downs through **Upper Beeding** to **Edburton**, **Fulking**, **Poynings** (pronounced Punnings) and **Newtimber** to **Pyecombe**, each with a typical downland church. This is a great drive running beneath **Devil's Dyke** (693ft/217m), one of the most popular Downland excursions in Victorian times and among other ways of reaching it was a funicular railway from Poynings to the top, where Devil's Dyke Hotel provides refreshments and a restaurant with good views. Today there is a car park for kite flyers and hang-glider hobbyists who approach it from the south. At the foot of these Downs the rain water that is washed from the slopes meets a non-porous strata and bubbles out of the ground, most notably at Fulking, where sheep used to be driven every year for a wash before being sheared. Those were lively times for the excellent Dog and Shepherd pub, which today still makes a good stop beside the bubbling water. A variety of local ewes' cheeses is on the menu and they make a convincing Downland ploughman's lunch.

Negotiating the A23, the road east beneath the Downs heads towards **Clayton**, but just before arriving in the village there is a lane on the right leading up to the **Jack** and **Jill windmills**. This unmissable couple have long been a landmark. Jack is black, a solid tower mill built in 1896 and privately owned. Jill is a white post-mill, built in Brighton in 1820 and hauled up here by oxen some 30 years later. Jill is open on Sundays through the summer and still grinds flour which can be bought.

Clayton itself has some of the finest early wall paintings in the church of **St John the Baptist** with ★ **frescoes** dating from around 1080. Above the chancel arch is Christ presiding over the Last Judgment and the narrative scene continues around the nave walls.

Beyond Clayton is ★★ **Ditchling**, an attractive Downs village at a crossroads where some inhabitants can remember playing dice without fear of motor traffic. The village is associated with the sculptor and typographer Eric Gill (1882–1940), and a number of other artists and craftsman, including Gill's teacher, Edward Johnston, whose block alphabet styled the whole London Transport system. A leaflet in **Ditchling Museum**, which has examples of their work, has a map with a village walk showing where they all lived (1 April to 31 October, 10.30am–5pm, Sundays 2–5pm; winter weekends only, or by appointment). Part of the museum, which has a collection of corn dollies and rural implements is housed in the old schoolmaster's cottage, where the first incumbent had 13 children and eventually emigrated to America. Descendants continue to return to their ancestral home.

To Ditchling's museum

The museum is at the back of the 13th-century church of **St Margaret's**, which contains a Norman treasure chest. These lands were part of the Ditchling royal stud, established in the 13th century by Edward I to breed war horses, and there was an annual horse fair here until the 19th century. Opposite the south entrance to the church is Wings Place, the most important of a number of interesting old houses in the village.

43

Ditchling Common, with nature trails, lies to the north of the village, and **Ditchling Beacon** rises to 813ft (248m) in the south. The road goes right by the summit where a dew pond lies. To the east, the road follows the humps of the downs beside fine flinty manor farms and by **Plumpton Agricultural College** which has a plant shop on weekdays, reached down a lane with a signpost to the church of **St Michael** which has the remnants of 12th-century wall paintings, contemporary with Clayton's. Plumpton National Hunt racecourse is near the railway station at Plumpton Green. The road ends at the A275 just outside Lewes (*see Route 7*).

View over Ditchling

Route 7

Lewes

Castle – Museum of Sussex Archaeology– Lewes House – The Old Needlemakers – Cliffe – Lewes Priory – Anne of Cleaves House – Southover Grange – Thomas Paine House

A day in Lewes

The county town of East Sussex (pop. 16,000) which spills down from the castle heights through riverine twittens to the banks of the Ouse is a centre for crafts and antiques. It has a radical core that nurtured the thoughts of Tom Paine and has inflamed the most incendiary bonfire nights in Britain. It provided Protestant martyrs and successfully fought the crown in both the 13th-century Barons' War, which resulted in the first House of Commons, and in the Civil War (1642–8).

Strategically well sited overlooking a gap cut through the Downs by the River Ouse, Lewes has been a pivotal town for many centuries. It was an important Saxon settlement, with two mints, and when the Normans arrived they built not only the impressive castle but also the huge monastery of St Pancras, which included a church the size of Westminster Abbey. Today, Lewes's continuing prosperity as a port and market town for the area, as well as the county town of all Sussex, is clearly evident in its many fine buildings.

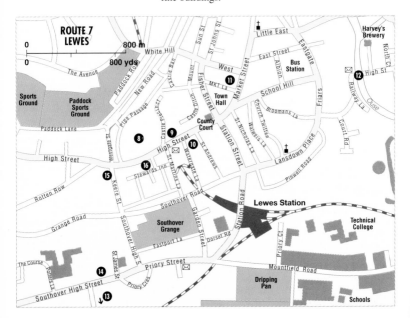

Undoubtedly the most exciting time to visit the town is on 5 November when Britain's biggest bonfire night takes place. Visiting cars are banned and the best way to get there is by special train from Brighton. The event recalls the Protestant martyrs and is still, on the surface, highly anti-Catholic, with effigies of the Pope burnt along with any current unpopular figures. The Bonfire Boys form societies in different parts of the town and on the night, dressed in costume, they march through the streets with rolling tar barrels, fire crackers and other incendiary devices. Their noisy passage ends with huge bonfires around the town and up on the Downs.

The ★★★ castle ❽ is the high point of the town. Tickets for combined visits are sold at the museum in the Tudor Barbican House in the High Street (10am–5.30pm, 11am–5.30pm Sundays and Bank holidays; admission fee, concessions for English Heritage members). The castle, built by the Conqueror's William de Warrene, and the 14th-century barbican gate should be scaled for views down to the Ouse estuary at Newhaven, across to Firle Beacon in the east, and Harry Hill in the west, site of the Battle of Lewes in 1264 when Simon de Montfort and the barons defeated Henry III, forcing him to sign the Mise of Lewes which brought parliamentary government to England. The bowling green at the foot of the castle used to be a jousting yard, and beside it is a diagram pointing out sites in the stages of the battle.

Barbican Gate and castle exterior

The ★ **Museum of Sussex Archaeology** ❾ forms part of the complex. It was once the property of Thomas Kemp who sold land to the Prince of Wales for the Royal Pavilion in Brighton to be built on, and his son developed Kemp Town. The museum gives an idea of the county's past and has an excellent audio-visual display based on a model of the town in 1870.

Streets down from the High Street on the right include a number of twittens and on the corner of Church Twitten is **Lewes House** ❿ (1812). Though now occupied by the council, it is worth contemplation, for here the anglophile New England art collector and aesthete Edward Perry Warren lived for 38 years from 1890 with a male 'brotherhood', building up the basis for the classical collections in the Boston Museum of Fine Arts and the Metropolitan Museum in New York. He also commissioned Auguste Rodin for a version of *The Kiss*, with the man's genitals 'to be seen in their entirety'. Though the French sculptor failed to comply entirely, the result horrified the Lewes town council when it went on display, and it can today be seen in The Tate Gallery in London.

Buskers in Lewes

On the River Ouse

Cliffe Bridge

The grandest building in the High Street is the neoclassical County Court (1812), which has Wisdom, Justice and Mercy personified on its facade. In the White Hart Hotel opposite innocence is celebrated and guilt bewailed after sentences are handed down. On the corner of Fisher Street is the Town Hall, the former Star Inn, dating from the 15th century. A plaque commemorates the 17 Protestant martyrs, who had been imprisoned in the inn's cellars and were burnt on this spot between 1555 and 1557. In the **Star Brewery** in Fisher Street there are daily demonstrations by potters, framers, bookbinders, woodturners and glassblowers. Crafts are on sale in the shops and stalls of **The Old Needlemakers** ⓫ in the adjacent West Street, the premises of a 19th-century candle and needle factory.

The High Street continues down to the Ouse, crossed by **Cliffe Bridge** ⓬ (1727). Just before it on the right is Riverside, an old commercial building with such stalls as Say Cheese, selling local produce, and Colin Staplehurst, an organic butchers. There is little evidence of the bustling riverfront this once was: the only sign of industrial activity today is the smoke coming from Harvey & Son, the Lewes brewery, remodelled in 1880. Their shop just over the bridge in Cliffe High Street sells their wares, including a Tom Paine ale, as well as wine and cider from all over Sussex.

On the Lewes bank, Friary Walk leads round to Southover High Street and St John the Baptist Church which, hard to imagine, was once part of ★ **Lewes Priory** ⓭ reached down Cockshut Street, the next turning left. It is worth first visiting ★★ **Anne of Cleves House** ⓮ on the opposite side of the road (25 March to 5 November

10am–5.30pm, Sundays 2–5.30pm; 6 November to 24 March, Tuesdays and Thursdays 10am–5.30pm, admission fee). This 16th-century timber-framed hall house was given to Anne of Cleves in her divorce settlement with Henry VIII, though she never came here. Rooms are furnished as they might have been in the 17th and 18th centuries and there is a collection of finds from the Priory.

The house is a starting point for a one-hour tour of the ruins (10 June to 9 July, weekends only at 2pm, 15 July to 3 September, daily 2pm and 3.30pm). From the ghostly remains left after Henry VIII's vandalous reformation, there is a merest hint that here was one of the finest collections of monastic buildings in Britain. Founded by William de Warenne in 1080, with the great abbey of Cluny as a model, it became one of the largest Cluniac monasteries in Europe. The remains of William and his wife Gundrada were excavated during the building of the railway in 1845, and were reburied in a neo-Norman chapel in St John's. Gundrada's 1160 tomb slab in black Tournai marble is a rare survivor from those times, and their discovery led to the formation of the Sussex Archaeology Society. Beside the ruins in the former herb garden is Enzo Plazzotzzotta's **Montfort Memorial** (1964), a bronze chaplet depicting various scenes from the Battle of Lewes. At the eastern end of the ruins is The Mount, a Neolithic site and a medieval salt pan known as the Dripping Pan, from which there are good views.

Anne of Cleves House

Montfort Memorial

Among a number of Sussex buildings founded on the plunder of the priory's Caen stone was **Southover Grange** (1572), where the diarist John Evelyn (1620–1706) lived while at school. Nursery schools and the registrar's office occupy the building today, and the grounds are open to the public.

Above it is the steep, cobbled **Keere Street**  where, it is said, the Prince Regent accepted a wager to drive a coach and four downhill. At the top of the street is an attractive 15th-century bookshop. On the right, on the opposite side of the street, is St Michael's, one of three churches by the Ouse that have round towers, now hideously covered in pebbledash. On the near side is **Bull House** (1450) where Thomas Paine (1737–1809) lived and worked as an excise officer from 1768. It was a tobacconist's then, and he married the owner's daughter, though his activities in the local Headstrong Club in the White Hart may have contributed to the brevity of the relationship. In 1774 the author of *Common Sense* and *The Rights of Man* sailed for America, where he took active part in the Revolution and briefly served as First Secretary of State for Foreign Affairs. The building is now the headquarters of the Sussex Archaeological Society.

White Hart Hotel, stamping ground of Thomas Paine

The garden at Monk's House

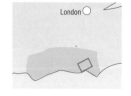

Route 8

Bloomsbury-on-Sea

Rottingdean – Newhaven – Monk's House – Glynde
Place – Firle – Charleston – Berwick – Drusilla's Zoo
– Michelham Priory – The Long Man, Wilmington –
Alfriston – Cuckmere Haven (30 miles/50km)

This is the literary route of the Sussex Downs, taking in
the homes of Rudyard Kipling, and of Virginia Woolf
and Duncan and Vanessa Bell, which gave this part of England the nickname of Bloomsbury-on-Sea. The area is centred on the meadowlands of the Ouse Valley, which lead
to the Sussex ferry port of Newhaven, and the Cuckmere
Valley, adjoining Seven Sisters Country Park. The two
valleys are divided by the high flat ridge of Firle Beacon, a favourite spot for paragliding. It is a musical route,
too, taking in Glyndebourne, the high point of the Sussex opera season.

In the Ouse Valley

Rudyard Kipling is associated with the attractive seaside
village of ★ **Rottingdean**, which lies 4 miles (6.5km) east
of Brighton beneath the smock mill (1802) on Beacon Hill,
and dissected by the main A259. He lived at The Elms,
an 18th-century house, from 1897 to 1902, when he wrote
Kim, *Stalky and Co* and the *Just So Stories*. In front of
the house his walled garden, formerly part of the village
green, is preserved for the public to enjoy.

Kipling's mother, Alice, was the sister-in-law of the pre-
Raphaelite painter Edward Burne-Jones (1833–98), who
lived in North End House in the west side of The Green,
where he had one of the rooms decorated like a bar in a
country pub. He designed windows in St Margaret's

Church, which were made up by William Morris's company in Merton. This Norman church was reworked by Gilbert Scott in 1856, and Burne-Jones's ashes were scattered in the graveyard and he is remembered in a plaque by the west entrance. Among tombstone inscriptions to the great and the good is 'The last Curtain Call for G.H. Elliott the Chocolate Coloured Coon'.

Burne-Jones window in St Margaret's church

Just south of the church and the village pond is The Grange, the former vicarage enlarged by Edwin Lutyens and once the residence of the artist William Nicholson (1872–1949). It is now the village library, and includes a small first-floor museum containing Kipling memorabilia as well as some of the fruits of the labours of Bob Copper, a local man who endeavoured to keep Sussex songs alive.

Although Rodmell lies just over the Downs, the only way to it is via **Newhaven**. This coast road, with the chalk Downs now turning into cliffs, is a rather dull – if short – run to the Channel port. It passes the depressing, utilitarian housing of **Peacehaven**, first called New Anzac-on-Sea when these 'homes for heroes' were built after World War I. **Newhaven Fort** (1860) is above the cliffs by the entrance to the harbour on the estuary of the Ouse. Covering 10 acres (4 hectares), it comprises barracks, magazines and tunnels, which contain militaria (April to October, Wednesday to Sunday 10.30am–6pm, daily in local school holidays).

49

The road that follows the west bank of the Ouse passes the pretty hamlets of **Piddinghoe** and **Southease**, both with unusual round towers in their ancient churches, which probably once served as watchtowers. The one at Piddinghoe also has a fine gold weathervane in the shape of a salmon. **Rodmell** is at the edge of The Brooks, the mead-

In a country churchyard

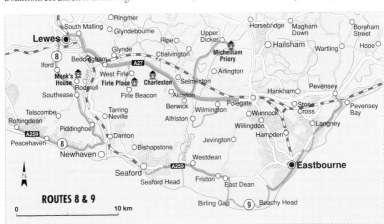

ROUTES 8 & 9

0   10 km

Bust of Virginia Woolf, Monk's House

ows that look across the river to Firle Beacon. One building in this village of sturdy thatched flint cottages is slightly out of place: ★ **Monk's House** is a weatherboard building dating from around the beginning of the 18th century (National Trust; 1 April to October 31, Wednesday and Saturday 2–5.30pm, last admittance 5pm; admission fee). After they were married in 1912, the writer Virginia Woolf (1882–1941) and her husband Leonard(1880–1969) lived in Asham House in what is now the chalk pits visible on the other side of the Ouse. They bought Monk's House in 1919. In the garden a fig tree now grows near the spot where Woolf had her writing outhouse. One morning in March in 1941 she set off across the meadows to the Ouse, filled her pockets with stones and drowned. Her ashes were buried in the garden and Leonard lived there until his death.

Looking over the fence that runs beside the lane leading to the pretty Norman church of St Peter, you can see the huge, bent mulberry trees that cover an old ice house.

The road continues up to Lewes and there is no way on to the A27 except to go through the town, following the signs to the town centre, and out again the other side. It may be noted that in 1919, wanting to move from Asham House, Virginia Woolf bought the Round House, a mill base, in Pipe Passage off Lewes High Street: she had not moved in when she realised she had made a mistake, and her attention was drawn to a poster advertising the auction sale of Monk's House.

Glynde Place

Two miles (3km) along the road towards Eastbourne, beneath the Bronze-Age hill fort of Mount Caburn, is a turning to **Glynde Place**. This Elizabethan manor, resplendent with clock tower and wyverns, has passed down through family hands for 800 years and now belongs to Viscount Hampden (May to September, Wednesdays, Thursdays and Sundays, 2–5pm, plus Easter Day and Bank Holidays; admission fee). It has a fine interior, lined with family portraits, including some by Kneller, Lily and Zoffany. There is a natural park with wide open views towards the Weald.

Glyndebourne

Next to the house is the Palladian church of St Mary, built in 1765 for one of the Hampden's predecessors, Richard Trevor, who was bishop of Durham. John Ellman (1753–1832) of Glynde Farm who was responsible for introducing the South Down breeds of sheep and cattle, is buried here, as is Audrey Mildmay, the opera singer who in 1934, with her husband John Christie, built the opera house at **Glyndebourne** a mile to the north. This was the Christie's Elizabethan family home and the intimate venue they created has become a part of the world opera season, greatly enlarged in 1994 by the bold and original design of Sir Michael and Patti Hopkins.

Less than a mile further along the A27 is the quiet downland village of **West Firle**, where **Firle Place** has been the
home of the Gage family since the 15th century. The original Tudor building, set in parklands at the end of a long
drive, was rebuilt in the 18th century in the present Georgian style. Among its treasures are paintings by Van Dyck,
Gainsborough and Reynolds in the Great Hall and Long
Gallery, and there is a good collection of English and
French furniture and Sèvres porcelain. As commander-in-
chief of the British army in America, Sir Thomas Gage
(1721–87) provoked the skirmish at Lexington and thus
the Revolution.

The church of St Peter has a stained-glass window by
John Piper, called *The Tree of Life*, dedicated in 1985 to
the late 6th Viscount Gage.

From the middle of the village a road goes up to **Firle
Beacon** (715f/t217m) where a giant in a silver coffin is
supposed to rest in a long barrow. Fires blazed from here
at the sight of the Spanish Armada, and now the slopes are
brightened by the chutes of paragliders.

The next stop along the A27 is ★★ **Charleston**, the
18th-century farmhouse made famous by Vanessa Bell
(1879–1961), Duncan Grant (1885–1978) and the Bloomsbury crowd. It is a fascinating place, with engaging hand-
painted panels and walls and redolent of the sparkling
crowd that once gathered here. Among its regular visitors were Dora Carrington, Lytton Strachey, Roger Fry
and John Maynard Keynes, as well as Bell's sister, Virginia Woolf.

Charleston's garden

51

Further work of Duncan Grant and Vanessa Bell and
their two children, Angelica and Quentin Bell, can be seen
at the 12th-century church of St Michael and All Angels
a couple of miles away at ★ **Berwick**. They were insti-
gated by Bishop Bell of Chichester, a champion of 20th-
century art, who turned to the artists when the church
was rebuilt after being damaged in the war. The church
had already once been saved from ruin by the energetic E.
Boys Ellman, who was curate from 1837–43, then rec-
tor from 1846–1906 and the author of *Recollections of a
Sussex Parson.*

Berwick Church

This is also a culinary corner: Middle Farm Shop on the
A27 has a wide selection of Sussex produce and incor-
porates the English Farm Cider Centre. Just beyond, at the
Alfriston roundabout, is The English Wine Centre, and
Drusilla's, a popular children's zoo (*see Practical Infor-
mation, page 77*).

Turn left at this roundabout for **Michelham Priory**
(April, July and September, 11am–4pm, May and June
11am–5pm, August 11–5.30pm). Just outside Upper
Dicker, this priory is attractively set on a 7-acre (3-hectare)

Michelham Priory

island on the River Cuckmere, which fills the longest moat in England and drives its watermill. It was built by Gilbert de Aquila in 1229 for the Augustinian order, and after it was dissolved in 1537 it was turned into a country house and farm. The Great Barn and Prior's Room serve as venues for concerts and exhibitions.

Local service

The next right on the A27 is **Wilmington**, famous for ★★ **The Long Man**, a 227-ft (70-m) tall figure inscribed in the side of Wendover Hill. Nobody knows who put this mysterious figure there, and there is no written record of it before 1779. A car park in the village is provided for those wanting to walk up to the site, where they will discover his proportion peculiarly elongated, for he is meant to be seen at an angle from below.

Wilmington had a priory from 1050 to 1413, and some of the monastic buildings remain. The church, which has a mighty and very ancient yew kept upright by great posts and chains, should be visited for its delightful 'butterfly' stained-glass window.

Alfriston Church

From Wilmington the road crosses the slender River Cuckmere to ★★ **Alfriston**, an attractive village of old pubs and tea shops long appreciated by walkers exploring the valley as the river meanders down to the sea. **Clergy House**, a thatched 14th-century Wealdon hall house is a focus on the village green (National Trust; April to end October, 10.30–5pm; admission fee). It was the first property acquired by the National Trust, in 1896. The church, which is raised on a mound, is built over an ancient burial ground.

The road beyond Alfriston leads to **Frog Firle Farm**, 462 acres (187 hectares) of the river valley and downland owned by the National Trust, and from here footpaths cut through the salt marshes and meadows of the estuary to reach the sea at **Cuckmere Haven**.

The meadows of the Ouse Valley

Route 9

Eastbourne

Eastbourne – Pevensey Castle – Beachy Head – Seven Sisters Country Park – Seaford *See map, p49*

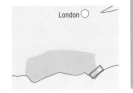
London

The crumbling chalk heights of the Seven Sisters and Beachy Head, rising 534ft (164m) above the English Channel, are where the South Downs reach a dramatic end. The whole of this part of coast, from sleepy Seaford to elegant Eastbourne, was the first stretch to be designated a Heritage Coast.

Beachy Head's lighthouse

Most of what the visitor will want to see in Eastbourne takes about four hours, and an excursion to Beachy Head and Seven Sisters can either be a 30-minute drive or, in fine weather, a pleasant day's walking and picnicking. Pevensey Castle, a 15-minute drive in the opposite direction and beyond the Downs, is also not to be missed.

History

The youngest of the south coast resorts, Eastbourne grew up under the patronage of the William Cavendish, 7th Duke of Devonshire, who was in possession of most of the land the town was developed upon. Saxons settled on the banks of the River Burne, and the old town grew up around the 12th-century church of St Mary. East Borne was first mentioned in the 16th century, when it had a population of around 800. By the time of the first royal visit in 1780, by the children of George III, the population had only risen to 1700.

53

Relic of a defensive past

During the Napoleonic wars, when the Martello towers were built along the coast, officers posted here to stand by for an expected invasion sent for their families and a society life began. Building on any scale did not, however, start until 1851. The Duke laid down policies that ensured this would be no town for the hoi-polloi, stipulating immaculate public parks and gardens, no seafront shops, and elegant hotel and apartment facades along the promenade all conforming to a certain style and all painted white. In 1883 the town received its charter. The council also bought up 4,000 acres (1,600 hectares) of Downland, which it manages today along with flocks of sheep.

Sights

★★ **Eastbourne** (pop. 84,000), home of lawn tennis, large conferences, schools and colleges, is one of Britain's stalwart resorts, attracting 20,000 students and 1.8 million visitors a year. It is a smart place, with 200 acres (81 hectares) of public gardens, signs on many bars about the way the clientele should dress, and chandeliers

Eastbourne

burning so brightly in the Grand Hotel that visitors may imagine this to be a rival of Monte Carlo.

It is not a difficult town to come to terms with: the centre, between the station and the pier, is pedestrianised and all the places of interest are well signposted. Ten minutes' walk north of the station is the **Old Town**, made up of a few timbered and flinty buildings, a pub and a church. **St Mary's** dates from the 14th century and is a fair size, reflecting the importance of the parish: several rectors of Eastbourne were treasurers of Chichester cathedral. The Lamb Inn next door is from the 14th century and has a vaulted crypt.

Towner House, a typical flint building of 1734 on the opposite side of the street, was the old manor house and now serves as the **Towner Art Gallery and Local History Museum**. The gallery has assembled an interesting modern art collection, which includes works of local scenes by Louisa C. Paris (1813–75) and Eric Ravilious (1903– 42), who died while on duty as a war artist during World War II.

Summer sun-seekers

Another reminder of the war is found in the 1938 church of **St Elizabeth** in Victoria Drive which was decorated with powerful Pilgrim's Progress murals by Hans Feibusch, who fled to Britain in 1933 and featured in Hitler's Degenerate Art exhibition.

The interesting parts of Eastbourne otherwise lie around Terminus Road in the pedestrianised shopping area, where The Sherlock Holmes is a hotter meeting place and Ziggy's is one of the popular nightspots, and by the Town Hall in South Street and Grove Road where there are good antique and secondhand bookshops.

Off Terminus Road is Cornfield Road and the **Tourist Information Office**. This leads to Cornfield Terrace and the ★ **Museum of Shops**, a four-storey town house (1850) fitted out with period shops brimming with nostalgia, and including such novelties as Edward VIII coronation souvenirs that never were. There is also a **Heritage Centre** in Carlisle Road, opposite Devonshire Park, which gives a history of the town.

Devonshire Park is the cultural zenith of the town. Eastbourne's Lawn Tennis Championships are held here just prior to Wimbledon each year, and the **Winter Garden**, **Devonshire Park Theatre** and **Congress Theatre** are energetic in putting on a wide range of entertainment all year round.

Teatime at the Wish Tower

A block away from here, on the seafront, are the Western Lawns and the **Wish Tower**, which tells the story of the 143 Martello towers along the coast, numbered east to west: this is No 73 (May to October daily, 10am–5pm, admission fee). The former lifeboat station is next to it, and this is now the **Lifeboat Museum** (May to October, free).

Eastbourne Pier

Eastbourne has had a lifeboat since 1822, and the boathouse was built in 1899 to house the last of the man-powered vessels. On the edge of the promenade is the Wish Tower restaurant and sun lounge, which offers customers the best panorama of the sea.

Redoubt lookout

The 3-mile (5km) promenade moves along Grand Parade past the classic bandstand to the pier (1866), where there are amusements halls, 10-pin bowling, bars and the Odyssey nightclub. Continuing along Marine and Royal Parades, the next clump of amenities is around another defensive installation, the ★ **Redoubt Fortress**, a moated circular fortress built in 1810 for a garrison of 350 men. A military museum in its casemates (Easter to November daily, 9.30am–5.30pm; admission free) has collections from the Sussex Combined Services, the Royal Sussex Regiment, the Queen's Royal Irish Hussars and the British Model Soldiers' Society. The Redoubt is a venue for spectacular '1812 Nights', military band concerts with fireworks, and wargame weekends are organised in the summer. The Orange Lily tea room is popular in the Redoubt, as is the nearby Edwardian Pavilion Tea Rooms, in which a good cup can be found.

Just beyond the Redoubt is **Treasure Island**, a children's adventure park and boating lake, and ★ **The Butterfly Centre**, a sub-tropical environment where it rains each morning to refresh the collection of 500 butterflies. (Easter to end October daily, 10am–5pm). **Fort Fun**, another adventure park with the Western as its theme is behind a suitable stockade further on (daily 10am–6pm), and close by is the **Sovereign Centre** leisure complex.

The new lifeboat station is along this shingle beach, as are some of the town's fishing boats, though many have now taken refuge in **Sovereign Harbour**, an ambitious development set to rival Brighton Marina. It occupies the Crumbles, a gravel area with a murky past of mur-

Pevensey Castle

ders and skullduggery, which now has a retail park of superstores. There is an outer, tidal harbour and an inner, tideless harbour reached through two locks. One of the first amenities to be set in place is The Earl of Zetland, a floating bar, restaurant and discotheque.

The flat land on this side of Eastbourne extends to **Pevensey Castle** (English Heritage; April to October, 10am–6pm; November to March, Wednesday and Sunday, 10am–4pm; admission fee), which claims to be the site of the landing of the Norman invading army of 1066. The Romans had been here first, and built a 10-acre (4-hectare) fort on what was an island at the mouth of the River Ashburn, with a port on its eastern side. The Romans called it Anderida and the fort was a protection against the Saxon pirates, who captured it in 490 AD not long after the Romans had left. By the time the Normans arrived and built a castle in the southeast corner of the site, it was known as Pevensey.

Much of the Roman wall, 30ft (9 metres) tall with 10 bastions, is still standing and freely accessible to visitors. The castle, which was given its curtain walls during the 13th century, was attacked on many occasions, but never breached. It gradually lost its importance as the sea receded.

At Wannock, on the northern outskirts of Eastbourne, is **Fliching Manor and Motor Museum**, a 15th-century hall house with a collection of arms and armour, gardens and more than 100 vintage racing cars. Memorabilia of the record-breaking Campbells includes their *Bluebird* speedboat. There is a also a go-kart track.

Beachy Head

Everyone staying in Eastbourne – as well as many people who are just passing through – visits ★★★ **Beachy Head**, a 10- minute drive past The Meads to the west. The drive is a delight, sweeping up above the town with fine views back over the pier, the promenade and the coast towards Dover, where the North Downs end in the less lofty White Cliffs.

The Beachy Head Countryside Centre (Easter to September, 10am–6pm), with the Brewer's Fayre restaurant and pub, lies just back from the precipitous edge of the cliff. It provides information about the geology and history of the area, together with details of its flora and fauna, which includes orchids and Adonis Blue butterflies. A 'talking shepherd' recalls the Downs rural past. From the top of the cliff, there is a view down to the red-and-white striped unmanned lighthouse. This awe-inspiring and perilous spot is also a favourite place for suicides and the Samaritans have a volunteer standing by.

Birling Gap, not far beyond Beachy Head, provided

the only access point to the beach anywhere along these cliffs. Because high tides cut off all access to the beach, it is important for walkers to consult tide tables and be sure they don't go down on the beach unless they can be sure of getting off again safely. In 1995, however, progressive cliff erosion made the steps at Birling Gap unsafe, and it is not certain whether they will be restored. Owners of the Birling Gap Hotel, which has a café overlooking the sea, believe they will have to organise their own dismantling before the end of the decade or else the sea will do it for them.

From Birling Gap the road turns inland towards East Dean, passing en route the **Sheep Centre** (March to September) which gives an inside view of sheep farming on the Downs.

Birds of a feather

57

The footpaths beyond Birling Gap lead over the Seven Sisters, undulant hills formed by river erosion, and named Haven Brow, Short Brow, Rough Brow, Brass Point, Flagstaff Point, Bailey' Hill and Went Hill. The 700-acre (280-ha) ★★ **Seven Sisters Country Park**, owned by the National Trust, has a centre at **Exceat Farmhouse** back on the main A259 just before it heads off across the Cuckmere Valley to Seaford. The centre, on the edge of Friston wood, has information about the park, a restaurant and bike hire facilities. Also here is **The Living World**, with vivariums of aquariums.

The first turning on the left on the far side of Exceat Bridge leads to the access point of the 303-acre (125-hectare) **Seaford Head Nature Reserve** which lies between Seaford Head and Cuckmere Haven.

The cliffs at Seven Sisters

Archaeology

Opposite: statue at Monk's House

During the construction of the Lewes to Brighton railway line in 1845, the coffins of William de Warenne and his wife Gundrada, a daughter of William the Conqueror, came to light. The discovery caused such interest that the Sussex Archaeological Society was formed.

There are few places in England that are so rich in archaeological clues to the past. Signs are here from the dawn of man, as revealed in the 1993 discovery at Boxgrove of a 500,000-year-old nomad hunter from the Mesolithic age, and the oldest Briton found to date. He was 6ft (1.8m) tall, weighed 13 stone (82kg) and ate rhino, bear, red dear and aurochs (cattle).

Boxgrove Man

Evidence of the first invading settlers comes from the dozen 'causeway' camps, earthwork enclosures the Neolithic tribes (5,000–4,000BC) built all along the Downs from Salisbury Plain. Four are on the South Downs: the Trundle, above Chichester, Barkhale above Bignor, Whitehawk above Brighton and Coombe Hill above Eastbourne. Several of their 'barrows' or burial grounds have been discovered, such as Bevis's Thumb in Compton and Windover Hill near Alfriston.

Farmsteads were settled during the Bronze Age, such as the one at Black Patch near Alciston, and at Itford Hill near Lewes, where 20 households were identified in excavations in 1956. Around the 3rd century BC large hill forts at the Trundle and Cissbury were built. At Cissbury, where a mile-long (2-km) wall enclosed a 60-acre (24-hectare) site, 150 flint mines have been found. Other forts, such as Mount Caburn, were strengthened against invasion. The Belgic tribes, who invaded in 75BC, left evidence of their civilisation in coin hoards, pottery and jewellery.

A stone in Chichester's Assembly Rooms, found in 1723, is dedicated by local shipbuilders to a temple of Neptune and Minerva, 'by the authority of Tiberius Claudius Cogidubnus, Great King in Britain.' Cogidubnus, a Belgic Celt who aided the Romans with their invasion in 54BC, is thought to be the builder of the Palace of Fishbourne, the largest domestic Roman building found in Britain, discovered in 1964. Under the Romans Chichester became a fortified town, but Pevensey was their main garrison post in Sussex, and the great defensive wall they built can still be seen.

The Palace of Fishbourne

Local museums, particularly at Chichester, Worthing, Brighton and Lewes, all attest to the archaeologists' work in this rich seam of ancient history. Though deep ploughing and urban encroachment have destroyed many clues to the past, there is no doubt there is still a lot more to come.

Sussex Archaeological Trust, Bull House, 92 High Street, Lewes, East Sussex BN7 1XH. Tel: 01273 486620.

Architecture and Art

The overwhelming image of South Downs architecture is flint. These stones in hues of grey, mined in the chalk seams close to the surface, are sometimes used as rubble in-fill, and are sometimes knapped (chipped) and laid in proper courses. To strengthen buildings, or merely as decoration, dressed blocks have been used as quoins or cornerstones. These stones may be sandstone from Caen, home of William the Conqueror, who brought his building material with him (the Tower of London is in Caen stone). Sometimes the two materials were mixed to give a chequerboard effect, as in the tower of Steyning church and Marlipins, the 14th-century toll-house in Shoreham.

Sussex thatch

Thatch is a common roofing material, growing to great thickness on such houses as Big Thatch in Rodmell. But imported slate was used, too, and oak shingles can occasionally be seen.

The architecture of the Saxons (495–1066) is one of Sussex's great treasures: around 60 churches have traces of the simple architecture which applied a century or so before the Norman invasion. The best example is Sompting parish church, with a Rhenish Helm spire capped with shingles, the only one of its kind in Britain. Some if its timbers date from the time it was built in 960. Boshum claims to predate it, and there was said to be a small monastery here even before St Wilfred landed in 681. The tower of this harbourside church was used as a place of refuge. Saxon towers were usually square and squat, though three along the Ouse, at Piddinghoe, Southease and Lewes, are round and may have been watchtowers.

Boshum Church

The Normans (1066–1135) rebuilt most existing churches, often with Caen stone, adding their decorated, rounded arches. Chichester Cathedral's nave and Steyning church are fine examples. Enchanting frescoes decorated the plaster, only to be obliterated during the Reformation, though some have been revealed in restorations, notably over the Saxon chancel in Clayton church. The Normans founded monasteries at Arundel, Boxgrove, Easebourne, Michelham, Wilmington and Lewes, where St Pancras was the largest Cluniac monastery outside France. None survived the Reformation.

Frescoes in St Michael's, Wilmington

The Tudor and Stuart (1487–1713) manors represent the great country-house age of building and Petworth, Parham, Firle and Glynde displayed the wealth of their owners. The ruins of Cowdray still show how it must have rivalled Hampton Court. St Anne's House in Bramber and Anne of Cleves' House in Lewes are among good half-timbered vernacular building of the time.

Georgian (1714–1830) and Regency (1811–20) architecture imposed an elegance on Chichester, Lewes and

Brighton, as well as on some country houses. Essentially neoclassical, the best examples are Uppark and Pallant House, Chichester, where the interiors can also be appreciated. The style contributed to the gentrification of the resorts with fine terraces, squares and crescents, such as Brighton's Royal Crescent, where porticoes, balconies and bow-fronted windows added a touch of class. Nash's Pavilion at Brighton was the height of Regency extravagance.

Victorian architecture (1837–1901) dominated the seaside towns, as the railways brought prosperity and visitors in great numbers. Many of the great hotels and entertainment venues, as well as the piers, come from this era.

Regency Square, Brighton

Art and artists

The Downs and the Sussex coast have produced no front-rank artists, but they have provided inspiration for many, and today there is a lively arts scene.

J.M.W. Turner (1775–1851) is associated with Petworth House, which he often visited, turning his prolific hand to paintings of both the interior and the parkland with its roe and fallow deer. Many of his paintings hang in the house, which has the largest art collection in the National Trust's care, amassed mostly by the 3rd Earl of Egremont who gave Turner a studio, now the Red Room. The pre-Raphaelite painter Sir Edward Burne-Jones (1833–98) is associated with Rottingdean, where he had a house in the last 18 years of his life. His modest legacy is the seven stained-glass windows in the church.

Section of Turner's 'Chichester Canal'

Eric Gill (1882–1940), the sculptor and typographer, was at the centre of an art colony in Ditchling, which is still a thriving village for the arts, and some of their work can be seen at the local museum. Gill sculpted the Stations of the Cross for Westminster Cathedral and *Prospero and Aerial* on Broadcasting House, London.

John Piper (1903–1992), a war artist, boldly brightened Chichester cathedral with his altar tapestry, and one of his stained-glass windows can be seen in the church in West Firle. Chichester Cathedral is almost like a modern art gallery, with a Chagall window, a Sutherland, Procktor and Nicholson. The nearby Pallant House also has an excellent modern art collection (*see Route 1, page 17*).

Another war artist was Eric Ravilious (1903–42) whose work is, along with that of Louisa C. Paris (1813–75), a find at the Towergate Gallery in Eastbourne.

'Burling Gap' by Louisa C. Paris

Brighton Art Gallery has a good collection of paintings, including work by Alma Tadema, Edward Lear and Duncan Grant. Its Art Deco collection, with Charles Rennie Mackintosh furniture and Claris Cliffe pottery is excellent. Further work of Duncan Grant and the Bloomsbury set can be seen *in situ* at Charleston and Berwick (*see Route 8, page 51*).

Literature

The writers most associated with the South Downs are Richard Jefferies (1848–87), W.H. Hudson (1841–1922), Rudyard Kipling (1865–1936) and Hilaire Belloc (1870–1953). All had a love of the hills, and wrote about them. Jefferies' natural histories are detailed accounts of rural life in the downs. His book *Wild Life in a Southern Country* (1879) was followed by *The Amateur Poacher* and *Wood Magic* (1881). Hudson, who was born in South America, wrote *Nature in Downland* (1900) and *A Shepherd's Life* (1910).

Kipling at The Elms in Rottingdean

62

Though both Jefferies and Hudson wrote mostly about the Wiltshire and Hampshire downs, they knew the South Downs, too, and both ended their days in Goring. Belloc was a fan of Hudson, and he himself wrote a travel book, *Sussex*, in 1906. He grew up in Slindon and from 1906 lived in Shipley where he bought the smock mill.

Kipling, the first English writer to receive the Nobel Prize, knew the Downs from the eight years he lived at Rottingdean, and subsequently just beyond them at Burwash. It was Kipling who described the 'blunt, bow-headed whale-backed Downs', and he wrote, too, of the smugglers on the coast: 'Watch the wall, my darling, as the gentlemen ride by.'

Another admirer of Jefferies was John Galsworthy (1867–1933), author of *The Forsyte Saga*, who lived his last seven years in Bury House, Bury, receiving his Nobel laureate in 1932. His ashes were scattered across Bury Hill. Anthony Trollope (1815–82), author of *The Barchester Chronicles*, spent the last two years of his life in South Harting. H.G. Wells (1866–1946) grew up at Uppark and went to school at Midhurst, where he also taught.

Many authors came to Sussex to write: Dickens and Thackeray visited Brighton, Darwin wrote *Origin of the Species* in one of the houses on Marine Parade. Oscar Wilde conceived of the name of John Worthing for *The Importance of Being Ernest*, which he wrote in the resort, inspiring an annual Wilde Weekend in the town in July.

Virginia Woolf (1882–1941) and her husband Leonard (1880–1969) lived in Monk's House, Rodmell, until her depressions, exacerbated by the war and the battles in the skies overhead, drove her to suicide in the Ouse. The rest of the Bloomsbury crowd collected at Charleston (*see Route 8, page 51*).

Perhaps the last word should be about the Sussex poet William Hayley (1745–1820), a popular character from Eartham who brought John Milton to stay at Felpham from 1801–03, where he wrote *Jerusalem*. The Poet Laureate Robert Southey said of Hayley: 'Everything about that man is good except his poetry.'

Woolf's room at Monk's House

Music and Theatre

The highlight of live culture in the south is the Brighton Festival, three days of events which take place in May. There is theatre at the Royal, concerts in the Dome and the Pavilion's sumptuous Music Room, performance and music in the Concorde Bar, pirate ships in the marina, and comedy in late night haunts such as the Zap club underneath the arches on the seafront. Artists open their studio doors, and so does Michelham Priory, an elegant concert venue which serves dinner, too. (Festival office, tel: 01273 713875.)

The Theatre Royal in Brighton (tel: 01273 328488) often has pre-West End productions and there are ice shows at The Brighton Centre on the seafront (tel: 01273 202881). The Gardner Centre by the university has a theatre and gallery (tel: 01273 685861).

The Festival Theatre in Chichester has been renowned for its excellence since its inauguration. Each season includes a varied programme of music, dance and opera. It has a winter and summer season, the latter running from April to October (tel: 01243 781312).

Chichester Theatre

The south coast resorts are dab hands at entertaining, even if the top names don't always get here. The Winter Garden is one of four theatres in Eastbourne (general enquiries: 01323 412000). It holds music competitions as well as performances, and provides a venue for the New Sussex Opera.

In Worthing, the Connaught (tel: 01903 235333) and Pavilion theatres (tel: 01903 820500) serve the town well, while the Assembly Hall is where the bands go.

The Priory Playhouse in Arundel is setting for a week-long summer festival (tel: 01903 883690), and St Nicholas church is used for recitals.

Picnic at Glyndebourne

Food and Drink

Opposite: rich man's table

'In the manner of eating I can only compare the Downland labourer to his favourite animal, the pig,' wrote Arthur Beckett at the turn of the century. 'His food, piled up on the plate, is often saturated with liquid from the cooking pot. He sets to work with a great smacking of lips and munching of jaws...The amount of food and drink that he will consume at a meal is astonishing, even for a man engaged all day in the open air.'

Garden plums

The ploughman, guiding his oxen all day, or the rheumy shepherd come down from the hills, would be full of fresh air from the Downs and the sea and their appetites were seldom modest. Good solid food was what they needed: dumplings, plum heavies (like plum duffs), drip pudding (Yorkshire pudding made with suet), suet meat pudding or ten-to-one potato and meat pie. Leftover pastry would be made into coager cakes, which could contain pork fat or currants or whatever else might give it a taste. But in fact they were more likely to eat cold boiled cabbage soaked in vinegar, and be quite content.

On the rich man's table would be more than enough, and there have been accounts of meals in Sussex in excess of 15 courses, including chicken stuffed with soused mackerel. The Royal Pavilion in Brighton has a menu from 1817 in which 100 dishes were offered at a banquet for Grand Duke Nicholas of Russia.

The food yielded up by the Downs has always been straightforward fare. Its mop-head Southdown sheep and mahogany red Sussex cattle, descendants of the Saxon ox, may not be so evident today, as new fashions, tastes and crosses alter the classic breeds introduced by John Ellman of Glynde Farm, but livestock is still fat on the land. There are pigs and rabbits a-plenty, too, and no excuse not to eat good local meat.

Today these ingredients are modified to suit modern tastes: Sussex Crumpy, Sussex Blanket Pudding, Sussex Pond Pudding, Tipsy Sussex Square, Downland Rabbit Pie, are dishes to make us feel part of the region's rich culinary tradition.

A great place for fish

Whatever the fare, what keeps the culinary tradition is good local ingredients. Thirty kinds of fish are landed along the coast through the year and good restaurants make a point of buying it locally: Dover sole, turbot and brill in the spring; skate, lemon sole, turbot, brill and squid in summer; Dover sole, skate, cod, conger eel and whiting in the autumn; whiting, cod and plaice in winter. Cockles come from Selsey, and inland, notably in Arundel, there is trout and mullet.

Other local bounty includes flour from mills at the Weald and Downland Museum or the water mill at Michel-

Pick your own

ham priory; tomatoes from Worthing; vegetables from the coastal plain around Chichester ('It is impossible for corn land and agriculture to be finer than these,' William Cobbett wrote in his *Rural Rides*); luscious fruits from Kent, the Garden of England.

Downland ewes' cheese has to be hunted out: Sussex Slipcote, soft cheese with garlic and herbs; Duddleswell, a nutty cheese; Lords of the Hundreds, an excellent strong dry cheese that needs beer or wine to accompany it.

Beer has always been the Sussex tipple, and in such traditional events as wassailing, in which trees were entreated to crop well, beer or cider were downed by the bucket. Harvey's brewery in Lewes produces a first-rate beer and their shop sells local brews and wines. Ballards Brewery in Rogate is a small local producer, and Kings & Barnes, made in Horsham, reaches a few pubs here. The English Cider Centre at Middle Farm on the A27 near Alfriston has around 100 varieties of cider and perry, and it also has a good variety of local produce. Among ciders are the well-established, successful Merrydown company, long associated with its wine-like strong, still cider. The innovative Gospel Green, near Petworth, have produced a champagne method cider.

Vineyards have yet to beat their continental neighbours but some are worth seeking out. Stop by the vineyards as you pass, and go to the English Wine Centre in Alfriston to see the full range. It has a small museum of viniculture in England and arranges tastings. For many years the owner, Christopher Ann, was involved with a regional food festival in Alfriston every September. This has now moved to the Winter Gardens in Eastbourne.

A typical Sussex pub

Restaurants
Country pubs are among the best places to find good food these days on the Downs. Traditional watering holes such as the Swan at Fittleworth, the Black Rabbit at Arundel, the Rose Garden and Alciston, and the Shepherd and Dog at Fulkington usually offer a convivial welcome with warming winter soups and pies, and summer salads.

Resorts offer more than fish and chips, but restaurants can reflect the seasonal ebb and flow of visitors. Brighton, with a year-round clientele has an enormous collection of inexpensive restaurants, most popular of which are Donatello's in the Lanes (3 Brighton Place) and Pinocchio's beside the Theatre Royal (22 New Road). Food For Friends in the Lanes (42 Market Street) is a vegetarian favourite. There are also such 'chains' as Brown's, Café Rouge and Pierre Victoire. Diners from Brighton often go to Church Street in Hove, which has a good selection of restaurants of all nationalities.

Eastbourne has a catering college which even teaches Spanish chefs how to cook good English food for their clientele on the *costas*. The college has a restaurant, which can be a novel eating experience (tel: 01323 730851).

In this selection, prices are for a two-course meal with house wine, per head: **£** = less than £20, **££** = £20–30; **£££** = £30 plus.

Amberley (Route 3)

£The Boathouse, Houghton Bridge, Amberley, West Sussex, tel: 01798 831059. This Edwardian boathouse has good views of the Arun Valley. Fresh fish is a speciality.

Bramber (Route 6)

££The Old Tolgate Restaurant, The Street, Bramber, near Steyning, tel: 01903 879498. Also a hotel, this award-winning restaurant has a good carvery.

Brighton (Route 5)

££The Sussex Arts Club, 7 Ship Street, tel: 01273 727371. Serves British food in the clubby atmosphere of a Georgian building. Reserve. **£The Regency Restaurant**, 131 King's Road, tel: 01273 325014. A popular seafront restaurant specialising in fresh local fish and seafood.

Al fresco dining in Brighton

Chilgrove (Route 2)

££White Horse Inn, Chilgrove, Nr Chichester, West Sussex, tel: 01243 535219. Country pub and restaurant with a long-standing reputation. Al fresco meals in summer. After-theatre meals for the Chichester crowd.

White Horse Inn

Eastbourne (Route 9)

£££Mirabelle Restaurant, The Grand Hotel, tel: 01323 4190771. It is hard to imagine a swankier setting than Eastbourne's best. But the cooking is good, too. Cheaper is the **££Garden Restaurant** (tel: 01323 412345), and you can include a slow shuffle to the resident band in the Chatsworth.

Jevinton (Route 8)

££The Hungry Monk, tel: Polegate 482178. In the Cuckmere valley, this restaurant has been having fun for a long time, producing recipe books based on its good local food.

Midhurst: (Route 3)

££Maxine's, Red Lion Street, tel: 0173 081 6271. In a half-timbered house next to the Swan Inn, Maxine's is an established husband and wife restaurant which has won accolades without being too pricey. Robert de Jager is the chef, and his wife Marti runs the front of house. Closed on Mondays.

Activity Holidays

The nature of the South Downs makes this a natural walking area, as well as a good place to learn how to paraglide. The coast provides great opportunities to learn how to fish and sail.

Hands-on at Earnley

Multi-activity centres

The Earnley Concourse offers an extraordinarily wide range of activity holidays. Set in 10 acres (4 hectares) of garden and parkland south of Chichester, there is full accommodation with restaurant and heated indoor pool. There are art studios, craft and kitchen workshops and computer room, and courses include languages, countryside music, history and countryside studies. The Earnley Concourse, Earnley, Chichester West Sussex PO20 7JL, tel: 01243 670392; fax: 01243 670832.

In Brighton, multi-activity holidays are run by Fourth Dimension, 13 Eskbank Avenue, Patcham, Brighton, East Sussex BN1 8SL, tel: 01273 506955, and the Trekking Company 55 Washington Street, Brighton, East Sussex BN2 2SR, tel: 01273 673677.

A restful option

Art courses

These are organised by the artist Keith Wallace at a dozen venues around the Cuckmere Valley. Their day or residential courses for no more than eight people, with local hotel and bed and breakfast accommodation. Wallace also runs workshops in Eastbourne. Send a stamped and addressed envelope for the current programme to The Studio, 18 Chestnut Drive, Polegate, East Sussex BN26 5AN, tel: 01323 483 879.

Fishing

Boats for deep sea fishing can be hired from Jetty 32 on Brighton Marina, and trips last from 8am to 5pm. Contact Fred Cox, Brighton Marine Boatman's Association, tel: 0181 647 8414 (evenings). For sea fishing, enquire at the Tourist Information Centres. Rod licences are needed for all inland waters (contact Sussex Fisheries Authority, Coast Road, Pevensey Bay, tel: 01323 762691).

Horse riding

For holidays, or just hacking on the South Downs, all ages and weights, with a free childminding service: Willowbrook Riding Centre, Hambrook Hill South, Hambrook, near Chichester PO18 8UJ, Tel 01243-572683

Only for the brave

Paragliding and hang-gliding

These are excellent ways of appreciating the Downs. Firle, behind Brighton, is a popular take-off point. Sussex College of Hang Gliding and Paragliding does five-night courses on each. Minimum age 16. 10 Crescent Road, Brighton East Sussex BN2 3RP, tel: 01273 609925.

Sailing
The sea provides a number of opportunities for activity holidays. One of the most pleasant places to learn to sail is Chichester Harbour, which is relatively safe as well as picturesque. Powerboat and year-round yacht courses, lasting from one to 14 days are offered by Chichester Sailing Centre in Chichester Marina (tel: 01243 512557; fax: 01243 512570). There is also a Sailing and Windsurfing School at Eastbourne (11 Wrestwood Avenue, Willingdon, Eastbourne BN22 OHA, tel: 01323 502674) and there is an annual boat show in July in Sovereign Harbour. Brighton hosts the annual British Windsurfing World Cup, often in frightening seas. Try your hand on a calmer day by renting from Sunhire Watersports Rental, 185 Kings Road Arches, Brighton, tel: 01273 323160, or at Hove Lagoon (tel: 01273 424842). The Newhaven and Seaford Sailing Club, based in Marine Parade, Seaford, runs RYA yachting and windsurfing courses on a quiet lake in Piddinghoe (tel: 01323 890077).

Testing the water

Walking holidays
The South Downs Way runs along the ridge of hills 108 miles (174km) from Eastbourne to Winchester, and though it is possible to make up your own itinerary for the walk, there are experienced operators who can make a holiday out of the trail.

Footpath Holidays organises two and three-night walks along the South Downs from Beachy Head to Ditchling Beacon and beyond (16 Norton Bavant, Warminster, Wiltshire BA12 7BB, tel: 01985 840049; fax: 01985 840853).

Footprints is the least expensive and most active operator in the area. Walks leader Keith McKenna's itineraries include a walk around Arundel, around the South Downs Way and the Downs Link walk between Guildford and Shoreham, plus a country house break near Steyning. Footprints of Sussex, 47 Hills Road, Steyning, West Sussex BN44 3QC, tel: 01903 814506.

Instep organises walks along the length of the South Downs Way, from Eastbourne to Winchester. The 108-mile (174-km) trek takes between eight and 10 days. It also offers a three-day walking holiday following a 33-mile (53-km) disused railway track linking the South Downs Way to the North Downs Way, from Bramber to Guildford. The 51-mile (82-km) Wey and Arun Canal walk, from Weybridge in Surrey to Amberley, takes five days. Instep Linear Walking Holidays, 35 Cokeham Road, Lancing, West Sussex, tel/fax: 01903 766475.

Striding out at Ditchling Beacon

Getting There

By road

The major resorts are reached from London or the M25 through fast main roads which cut through the Downs: the A29 to Chichester, A24 to Worthing, A23 to Brighton, A22 to Eastbourne. Brighton is 50 miles (80km) from London and the nearest resort. The journey from London takes about 75 minutes, providing traffic is fairly light.

Passengers arriving by car through the Channel Tunnel, near Folkstone (Le Shuttle: tel 0990 353535), and the ferry port of Dover will pick up the A27 which runs all along the south coast.

Come by road or rail

By rail

There are direct rail services from London Victoria to Chichester, Worthing, Brighton and Eastbourne, and most of these pass through Gatwick. Trains run regularly from Gatwick to Brighton, taking 30 minutes. The Capital Coast Express runs from London to Brighton in less than one hour. Thameslink has regular trains from Bedford and stations between there and King's Cross, and there are direct InterCity Cross Country trains from the Midlands, the Northwest and Scotland.

Main rail enquiry line: tel: 0171 928 5100. Engineering work sometimes takes place at weekends and can disrupt journeys. It is worth checking before travelling, tel: 01273 206755.

The Eurostar train stops at Ashford in Kent, and although connections are promised to Brighton, it may still be best to go via Waterloo and Victoria stations in London (tel: 0345 881881).

By coach

There are regular coach services from London Victoria Coach station and fares are cheaper than rail fares. For information, tel: 0171 730 0202. The coach takes about two hours from London to Brighton, slightly longer to the other resorts.

By sea

Newhaven is the only Channel port in Sussex, and ferries go from here to Dieppe (tel: 01233 647047). Portsmouth, 30 minutes from Chichester, has sailings to Cherbourg (01752 221321 and 01705 772244). Dover, about an hour's drive east of Eastbourne, is the shortest Channel crossing, to Calais.

Dover offers the shortest hop from the Continent

By air

Gatwick Airport has direct rail links to Brighton and Worthing. Tel: 01293 535353.

71

Getting Around

By rail

A coastal service connects the towns along the coast from Portsmouth to Ashford: Bosham, Fishbourne, Chichester, Barnham, Bognor Regis, Ford (for Arundel and Amberley), Littlehampton, Angmering, Goring-by Sea, Durrington-on-Sea, West Worthing, Worthing, East Worthing, Lancing, Shoreham-by-Sea, Southwick, Fishergate, Portslade, Aldrington, Hove and Brighton.

From Brighton: London Road, Moulsecoomb, Falmer. Lewes (for Southease, Newhaven Town, Newhaven Harbour, Bishopstone and Seaford), Glynde, Berwick, Polegate, Hamden Park and Eastbourne. From Eastbourne: Pevensey & Westham, Pevensey Bay and on to Bexhill, Hastings and Ashford, where you change for Folkstone and Dover. Enquiries: 01273 206206755.

By bus

An easy way to see the sights

There are bus services throughout the area, though services between towns are irregular. Urban services are better, and those in Brighton are cheap and offer various multi-use ticket schemes in town and to outlying places. Tourist Information offices can usually dispense free bus timetables.

West Sussex: the Chichester, Worthing and Arundel areas are served by Stagecoach Coastline buses, tel: 01903 237661/10243783251.

Brighton is served by the Blue Bus Company (tel: 01273 886200) and the red and yellow buses of Brighton and Hove Bus Company (tel: 011273 674881). East Sussex: Stagecoach South Coast buses serve the Lewes and Eastbourne areas, tel: 0345581457. The Local Rider services are run by the County Council on uncommercial routes (tel: 01273 474747).

Jetlink is a bus service between Brighton and Gatwick Airport, tel: 0181 668 7261.

Tourist Information Centres can also often book local coach excursions.

By road

Finding a place to park

The main road through the South Downs is the A27, which bypasses all the main towns. A scheme to widen the eastern end around Firle is the subject of controversy. All main roads have a continual flow of traffic, but once off them into the Downs, they can seem a long way away.

Parking: In nearly all cases it is best to use car parks, which are plentiful in the main centres and in walking distance of all the sights and amenities. Short Stay car parks are usually more centrally sited and cost slightly more than

Long Stay parks. Parking wardens are particularly efficient in Brighton. Voucher parking systems operate in the larger towns, such as Brighton and Chichester. Voucher Parking Zone areas are clearly indicated on pavement signs. Parking meters also operate in towns, and pay-and-display car parks are generally the norm in most of the smaller towns, so it is a good idea to keep some change in readiness.

Brighton operates a Park and Ride scheme, with car parks located at Withdean Stadium, Lewes Road and Saltdean Lido.

Many car parks and other strategic places in Brighton and Eastbourne have coin-operated machines dispensing useful town plans.

By bicycle

For freewheelers

The South Downs offer good, if hilly countryside for bikers. Bikes can be taken free by rail across the area, and bridleways, including the South Downs Way, are open to bikers. A south coast cycle route has been designated along the coast from Worthing to Shoreham.

Bikes can be hired in Brighton at: Alpine Cycle Hire, 7 Beaconsfield Road, tel: 01273 625647, On Your Bike, 126–7 Queen's Road, tel: 01273 821369, and Sunrise Cycle Hire, West Pier Promenade, Kings Road, tel: 01273 748881; in Lewes at: Take A Ride, Barcomb Mills Station, tel: 01273 400950.

By boat

Chichester Harbour Water Tours are organised by Peter Adams, 9 Cawley Road, Chichester West Sussex PO19 1UZ, tel/fax: 01243 786418. Boats leave from Itchenor and the trips last around 1½ hours.

Chichester Harbour Water Tours

Arun Cruises run daily trips along the River Arun, from Littlehampton to Arundel and Amberley, from Easter to the end of September, tel: 01243 265792/01903 774808 for further details.

At Eastbourne, Bluebird Speedboats operate trips from the pier.

The Channel time from Newhaven to Dieppe has been reduced to around two hours, making it possible to have a day's outing in the French port (tel: 01233 647047).

Goodwood Pleasure Flights

Air trips

Goodwood Aerodrome near Chichester offers sightseeing helicopter tours (either set tours or go where you like) seven days a week, tel: 01243 530165. Fixed wing pleasure flights are organised by Goodwood Flying School, tel: 01243 7746556. A number of operators offer flights at Shoreham airport: Air South (tel: 01273 462874); Southern Air Ltd (tel: 01273 461661).

73

Facts for the Visitor

Events

There are carnivals, birdman competitions, and all manner of entertainments in the seaside towns throughout the summer. Also look out for open-air concerts at some of the great houses such as Parham, Petworth and Michelham Priory, and steam fairs, held throughout the region.

Full steam ahead

May: Brighton Arts Festival.
June: London to Brighton Cycle Ride. Tennis championships, Eastbourne. Corpus Christi flower carpet, Arundel Cathedral. Festival of Speed, Goodwood.
July: The Chichester Festival. Oscar Wilde weekend, Worthing.
August: Air show, Shoreham. National Bowls Championships, Worthing. Festival week and Festival Fringe, Arundel. English Wine and Regional Food Festival, Eastbourne.
September: Sheep fair, Findon.
November: London to Brighton Veteran Car rally.

Visitors' tickets

National Trust members have free entry to Petworth House, Uppark, Alfriston Clergy House and Monk's House, Rodmell.

The **Sussex Archaeology Society** has a 'Remains to be Seen' season ticket which allows entry to six 'Sussex Past' properties: Anne of Cleves House and Castle and Museum, Lewes; Fishbourne Roman Palace; Marlipins Museum in Shoreham; Michelham Priory and the Priest House in West Hoathly (not covered in this book). It also allows half price entry into **English Heritage** properties in Sussex.

Sussex Past, Barbican House, 169 High Street, Lewes, Sussex BN17 1YE

Hospitals

Chichester: St Richard's Hospital, Spitalfield Lane, tel: 01243 787970.
Brighton: Sussex County Hospital, tel: 01273 696955. Brighton General Hospital 01273 696011. Sussex Aids Centre, Brighton, tel: 01273 608511.
Eastbourne: King's Drive, tel: 01323 417400.

Phones

Keeping in touch

Telephones accept coins and phone cards, available from shops and post offices in various denominations. For international direct dialled calls (IDD), first dial 00 . Calls are cheaper after 8pm and at weekends. For direct (reverse charge) calls, dial 100 (inland), 155 (abroad).

Emergencies
Tel. 999 (ask for police, ambulance or fire service).

Tourist information centres
Arundel: 61 High Street, tel: 01903 882268
Bognor Regis: Belmont Street, tel: 01243 823140
Brighton: 10 Bartholomew Square, tel: 01273 323755
Chichester: 29a South Street, tel: 01243 775888
Eastbourne: 3 Cornfield Road, tel: 01323 411400
Lewes: 187 High Street, tel: 01273 483448
Littlehampton: Windmill Complex, Coastguard Road, tel: 01903 713480
Petworth: Market Square, tel: 01798 343523
Worthing: Chapel Road, tel: 01903 210022

Cricket
Sussex Country Cricket ground is in Hove

Golf courses
Around **Chichester**: Chichester Golf Centre, Hunston Village, tel: 01243 536666; two 18-hole courses; any day by arrangement. Cowdray Park, Midhurst, tel: 01730 813599;18 holes; Monday, Wednesday, Thursday. Goodwood, tel: 01243 774968;18 holes; any time by arrangement. Goodwood Park, tel 01243 775987; 18 holes; weekdays. Osiers Farm, London Road, Petworth, tel: 01798 344097; 18 holes; any day.

On the green

Around **Worthing**: Avisford Park, Arundel, tel: 01243 554611; 9 holes; any day. Hill Barn, Worthing, tel; 0903 237301; 18 holes; any day. Rustington Golf Centre, tel: 01903 850786; 18 holes; any day, book seven days ahead.

Around **Brighton**: Benfield Valley, Hove, tel: 01273 411358; 11 holes; pay-and-play any day. Brighton & Hove, Dyke Road, Brighton, tel: 01273 556482; 9 holes; most days. East Brighton, Roedean Road, Brighton, tel: 01273 604838; 18 holes; weekdays. Hollingbury Park, Ditchling Road, Brighton, tel: 01273 552010; 18 holes, Thursday. Lewes, Chapel Hill, tel: 01273 483474; 18 holes; any day. Pyecombe, Clayton Hill, tel: 01273 845372; 18 holes; Monday, Wednesday, Thursday. Waterhall, Patcham, tel: 01273 508658; 18 holes; any day.

Around **Eastbourne**: Eastbourne Downs, East Dean Road, tel; 01323 720827; 18 holes; Tuesday to Friday. Eastbourne Golfing Park, Lottbridge Drive, tel: 01323 520400; 9 holes; pay-and-play any day of the week. Royal Eastbourne, Paradise Drive, tel: 01323 729738; 27 holes; every day: afternoon only on Tuesday Wednesday and at weekends. Seaford, Firle Road, tel: 01323 892442; 18 holes; Monday, Wednesday and Thursday. Seaford Head, Southdown Road, Seaford, tel: 01323 894843; 18 holes; weekdays only.

Greyhound racing
A popular night out is at the Coral Greyhound stadium in Hove (tel: 01273 204601).

Horse racing
The South Downs provide natural settings for some of the finest race courses in the country. Glorious Goodwood is at the beginning of August, but there are other meetings from May to October. From March to September there is flat racing at Brighton Racecourse on Whitehawk Down, Kemp Town. The National Hunt race track at Fontwell has an unusual figure-of-eight track (closed June and July) and Plumpton has fixtures throughout the year.

Polo
Cowdray Park, Midhurst. Matches every weekend from April to September. Parking charge but entrance is free.

Stoolball
A forerunner of cricket, with teams from Midhurst, Rogate, Lurgashall, Lodsworth and Petworth.

Swimming pools
Most large towns have indoor pools and leisure centres. There is an open-air heated pool in Arundel, end of May to 1 September, 10am-5.30pm daily.

Walking and cycling
Leaflets on walks are available at Tourist Information Centres. *Exploring Sussex* is a useful booklet, giving some 200 walks and cycle rides in East Sussex. For bike routes in West Sussex contact local tourist office or Cyclists' Touring Club, West Sussex District Association, 65 Grand Avenue, Worthing, West Sussex, tel: 01903 501088.

Water babies

For Children

The beach is a natural place for children and the beaches west of Brighton are all fairly safe. Remember, however, that waves do have an undertow and the sea should be treated with respect. Small children are better off swimming not at high tide, when the incline is invariably deeper and the waves bigger, but when the tide is half-way out.

Bognor Regis has the Butlin's South Coast World, a successful family entertainment spot, with a pool and rides, which is also residential. Church Farm Holiday Village in Pagham is a smaller residential establishment, with entertainment laid on and its own lakes for watersports.

Harbour Park in Littlehampton can keep children occupied for a few hours. Garden Paradise just outside Newhaven, has a small dinosaur park among its attractions. In Eastbourne Fort Fun and Treasure Islands are the places to go. Other spots children will enjoy are the Amberley Museum, The Weald and Downland Museum, Singleton, and Drusilla's Park, Alfriston, which has excellent facilities and entertainments for a half day out.

During the summer holidays a number of activities on the coast are organised by Oscar the Octopus, a device for grouping together things to do for children aged between six and 16, from face painting walks to archery. For a current catalogue, tel: 01903 716133.

Karting There are tracks at Brighton Marina, Fort Fun in Eastbourne, and at Fliching Manor and Motor Museum just north of Eastbourne.

Burning up energy

Railways: Eastbourne: Miniature Steam Railway runs at Southborne Lake, Eastbourne. The Volks Electric railway from the pier to the marina in Brighton is the most famous seafront vehicle. A miniature steam train winds through the parklands at Bentley, a Tudor farmhouse north of Lewes, where there is an impressive wildfowl collection as well as vintage cars. There is a miniature steam train and an adventure playground. Sheffield Park is also just north of the Downs, but within easy reach. This is where the famous Bluebell Line runs up to Kingscote near East Grinstead, taking around 40 minutes each way.

Wildlife: Four activity stations at Arundel Wildfowl and Wetlands Centre are staffed on weekends in summer and during local school holidays from April to August. Stoneywish Country Park near Ditchling has a pets' corner, farm animals and wildfowl lakes.

Sussex Falconry Centre offers opportunities to see and handle falcons. Locksacre Aquatic Nursery, Wophams Lane, Birdham, near Chichester, take the Wittering turning off the A27. Tel: 01243 512472.

Accommodation

There is plenty of accommodation, from the Grands in Brighton and Eastbourne to myriad Sea Views on the coast. Most small towns have a principal inn with beds which, along with B&B farmhouses, make the most attractive places to stay.

B&Bs are plentiful

There are often special offers available on winter or weekend breaks, and it is always worth asking about them when booking.

Tourist Information Offices have full lists and for a minimal fee, will book ahead on your behalf. Thomas Cook has an accommodation bureau in Brighton station. In Chichester from April to October 'Overnighter' short breaks include the theatre and accommodation (for details, tel: 01243 539435).

Grand Hotel, Brighton

This is not a list of the best – the Grand Hotels of Brighton and Eastbourne, Shelleys in Lewes and Amberley Castle are beyond most people's purses. Nor does it include some of the cheapest – bed and breakfast in some of the resorts can be had for less than £15 a night. But they should give a flavour of each route.

Price Guide: **£**=less than £25 per person per night, **££**=£25–35 a night, **£££**=£35 plus.

Alfriston (Route 8)

££The George Inn, High Street, Alfriston, East Sussex BN26 5SY, tel: 01323 870319. Dating from the 15th century, this pub and hotel is in the middle of this popular village. Has four-poster beds and an inglenook in the restaurant where local fresh fish are a speciality.

Arundel (Route 2)

££Dukes, 65 High Street, Arundel, West Sussex BN18 9AJ, tel: 01903 883847. An elegant town house built in 1840. All bedrooms have bathrooms. Fine Italian walnut ceiling in the dining room where a full English breakfast is included. The restaurant is open every day.

Brighton: (Route 5)

£££The Old Ship Hotel, King's Road, Brighton BN1 1NR, tel: 01273 329001; fax: 01273 820718. One of the oldest in Brighton: elegant, traditional, but not too grand. **££The New Madeira Hotel**, Marine Parade, Brighton, East Sussex BN2 1TL, tel: 012723 698331; fax: 01273 606193. Ask for a room at the front, with a bay window, to have a view of the bright lights of the pier. Weekend break special rates. **£The Grapevine**, 30 North Road, Brighton BN1 1YB, tel: 01273 681361. This is a good basic bed-and-breakfast and café in the middle of the bustling North Laine.

Chichester (Route 1)
££Suffolk House Hotel, 3 East Row, Chichester West Sussex PO19 1PD, tel: 01243 778899, fax: 01243 787282. Privately-run hotel in a fine Georgian building, with restaurant and small garden. **The Millstream Hotel and Restaurant**, Bosham, Chichester, West Sussex, tel 01243 573234. Quiet country hotel near Bosham harbour with various rosettes and merits for its food and hospitality.

Eastbourne (Route 9)
££Sea Beach House Hotel, 39–40 Marine Parade, Eastbourne, East Sussex, tel: 01323 410458. Built in 1790, this seafront hotel is an unusual Regency town house, where Alfred Lord Tennyson twice stayed. **££De Vere Grand Hotel**, King Edward's Parade, Eastbourne, BN21 4EQ, tel: 01323 412345, fax: 01323 412233. All amenities, including indoor and outdoor pools. Trained nannies on hand at holiday times.

De Vere Grand

79

Findon (Route 6)
££Findon Manor Hotel, High Street, Findon, West Sussex BN14 OTA, tel: 01903 872733, fax: 01903 877473. Attractive flint manor house with bar and restaurant, rooms with four-posters and Jacuzzis.

Lewes (Route 7)
£££The White Hart Hotel, High Street, Lewes, East Sussex BN7 1XE, tel: 01273 473794. Run on modern lines, but full of history and with an indoor pool. **££The Crown**, Market Street, Lewes, East Sussex BN7 2NA, tel: 01273 480670. Bed-and-breakfast in an old town inn, with a fine Venetian window over the entrance.No restaurant.

Midhurst (Route 3)
£££Angel Hotel, North Street, Midhurst, West Sussex, GU29 9NH, tel 812421. Dates from 1420. Hilaire Belloc called this 'the most revered of all prime inns in England.' Features include Tudor bread ovens, a wig closet, fine Jacobean hall and four-poster beds in some rooms.

Steyning (Route 6)
££Springwells, High Street, Steyning BN44 3GG, tel 01903 812 446, fax: 01903 879823. An upmarket bed and breakfast in a Georgian mansion, with walled gardens and pool. Breakfast menu includes kippers, haddock and porridge made with whisky, brown sugar and cream.

Springwell Hotel, Steyning

Worthing (Route 4)
££Burlington Hotel, Marine Parade, Worthing, West Sussex BN11 3QL, tel:01903 211222; fax: 01903 209 561. Built in 1864, overlooking gardens and the sea.

Index

Alfriston.................................52
Amberley...........................26–7
Amberley Museum....................26
Anne of Cleves House.............47
Arundel.............................27–28
Arundel castle.........................27

Beachy Head.........................56
Beachy Head Countryside
    Centre.............................56
Berwick.........................51, 61
Bignor Roman Villa.................26
Birling Gap.........................56
Bognor Regis.........................29
Booth Museum.......................38
Bosham.............................20
Boxgrove.............................21
Boxgrove Man...................21, 59
Boxgrove Priory......................21
Bramber.............................42
Brighton.............................33–9
    Brighton Museum and Art
        Gallery........................37
    Fishing Museum.................39
    Lanes, the.......................38
    marina............................39
    North Laine......................35
    Palace Pier......................39
    Royal Pavilion...............36–7
    Sea Life Centre.................39
    St Nicholas.......................38
    St Peter's.........................35
    Sussex Toy and
        Model Museum..............35
    Theatre Royal....................38
    Volk's Museum..................39
Broadwater.........................30
Bury.................................26

Chanctonbury Ring..................41
Charlston.....................51, 61, 62
Charlton.............................23
Chichester.........................16–20
    castle..............................17
    Cathedral......................18–19
    Chichester District Museum....17
    Festival Theatre.................17
    Pallant House....................17
    Priory Park.......................17
    St Mary's Hospital...............17
    St Olave's.........................17
Chilgrove.............................24
Chilsdown Vineyard.................23
Cissbury Ring.........................40
Clayton.........................42, 60
climate..................................6
Climping Beach......................29
Cowdray House......................25
Cowdray Park.........................25
Cuckmere Haven....................52

Devil's Dyke.........................42
Ditchling.............................42–3
Ditchling Beacon.....................43
Ditchling Common...................43
Drusilla's.........................51, 77

Easebourne.........................25
Eastbourne.........................53–7
    Devonshire Park.................54
    Old Town..........................54
    Pevensey Castle.................56
    Redoubt Fortress................56
    St Elizabeth......................54
    St Mary's.........................54
    Towner Art Gallery and Local
        History Museum............54
    Wish Tower.......................54
East Dean.............................23
East Preston.........................30
Edburton.............................42
English Martyrs Church,
    Goring............................30

Ferring.............................30
Findon.............................40
Fishbourne Roman Palace.........19
Firle Beacon.........................51
Firle Place.........................51
Fittleworth.........................26
Fliching Manor and Motor
    Museum...........................56
Frog Firle Farm.....................52
Fulking.............................42

Gill, Eric.............................61
Glyndebourne.......................50
Glynde Place.........................50
Goodwood House...................22
Goodwood racecourse.............22
Goring.............................30

Halnacker windmill.................21
Highdown Chalk Gardens.........30
Highdown Hill.......................30
Hove.................................39
Hudson, W.H..................30, 62

Jack and Jill windmills.............42
Jefferies, Richard...................62

Kipling, Rudyard.............11, 62

Lancing College Chapel............32
Lewes.............................44–7
    Anne of Cleves House.......46–7
    castle..............................45
    Cliffe Bridge.....................46
    Lewes House......................45
    Museum of Sussex
        Archaeology................45

The Old Needlemakers...........46
    Star Brewery.....................46
Littlehampton.................29–30
Long Man, the.......................52

Marlipins.........................32, 60
Michelham Priory...................51
Midhurst.........................25–6
Military Aviation Museum,
    Tangmere.........................21
Monk's House.......................50

North Marden.......................24
Newhaven.............................49
New Timber.........................42

Parham House.......................27
Peacehaven.........................49
Petworth.............................26
Pevensey Castle.....................56
Piddinghoe.........................49
Piper, John.........................61
Plumpton.............................43
Preston Manor.......................39
Pyecombe.............................42

Rodmell.............................49
Rottingdean.........................48
Rustington.........................30

Seaford Head
    Nature Reserve..................57
Seven Sisters Country Park......57
Sheep Centre.........................57
Shoreham Airport...................32
Shoreham-by-Sea...................32
Singleton.............................23
Sompting.............................31
Southease.............................49
South Harting.......................24
Southover Grange...................47
Steyning.........................41–2, 60

Tangmere.............................21
Tarring.............................31
Trundle.............................22
Turner, J. M. W.....................61

Uppark.............................24
Upper Beeding.......................42

Weald and Downland Open-air
    Museum...........................23
West Dean Gardens.................23
West Firle.........................51
Wildlife and Wetlands Centre,
    Arundel...........................28
Wilmington.........................52
Woolf, Virgina.................51, 62
Worthing.........................31–2